DISCOVERING INDIA

DISCOVERING INDIA

KAROLINA GOSWAMI

Vitasta

Published by
Renu Kaul Verma
Vitasta Publishing Pvt Ltd
2/15, Ansari Road, Daryaganj
New Delhi-110 002
info@vitastapublishing.com

ISBN 978-93-86473-78-3

First Edition 2020
MRP ₹595

The content in this book has been made available for educational and informational purposes only, and is not intended to be a substitute for a professional advice. The sources which have been used to present the data, facts, and statistics have been mentioned. The author has made every effort to present information that is accurate.

Editor: Papri Sri Raman
Cover and layout: Somesh Kumar Mishra
Printer: Chaman Enterprises

Contents

How It All Started...

There are only a couple of states in India which I have not visited yet. I am fortunate to have travelled very extensively in India and in the process, I have experienced countless precious moments while meeting and interacting with thousands of amazing souls, many of whom I will never forget.

But the actual journey began in 2014.

In 2014, I visited India for the first time. On my very first trip, I was blessed to have the opportunity to go on a road trip of more than 10,000 km bisecting the country's rural and urban sides. We were a group of four friends – three Polish nationals and one Indian. We spent months travelling across the country. That was a very intense and educational experience. Probably, it was during this trip when India started to deeply affect my inner senses. I went back to Poland, but it wasn't the same anymore.

By 2015, Anurag and I had known each other for nearly two years and we finally decided to marry.

My parents, siblings and friends wholeheartedly supported my decision to marry a Hindu Indian man; however, some people objected very strongly. The primary reason was that Anurag was a Hindu. For some of them, Hindus were devil worshipers, demonic or Satan related. The relatives who objected were regular church goers and believed that they were true Christians.

In addition, some people even warned me that I would be burnt alive or raped in India. Some said that a Hindu man has many wives. Some said that at the end of the day, the marriage with Anurag is not totally bad as his complexion is not that dark.

On the other hand, in India, the situation was very welcoming. Anurag belongs to a very Dharmic Hindu family and they wholeheartedly welcomed his decision to marry a Christian girl. From day one, I was showered with genuine affection and respect, not only from his immediate family members but also from his relatives.

We decided to have two wedding ceremonies – one in India (with Hindu customs) and one in Poland (with Christian Catholic customs).

Soon, the dreams of my parents to have a traditional Christian wedding for their daughter came crashing down as the church in Poland denied me permission to have my wedding rituals conducted in the church.

The reason behind this was an absolute shocker.

Since I was marrying a Hindu man, the church in Poland wanted me and my future husband to submit a signed written confirmation that we will raise our (to be born) children only as Christians.

The idea of declaring the religion of an 'unborn child' did not appeal to us and we both refused to agree. As a result, the church did not participate in our wedding ceremony in Poland and we could not get married in the church.

On top of that, some of my relatives refused to attend our wedding because I was marrying a Hindu. However, I must mention that my parents and siblings always stood by my side and were genuinely supportive of our marriage.

On the other hand, all the Indian guests joyfully attended our wedding celebrations that took place in India. Immediate family members, friends, relatives or even neighbours...nobody bothered to ask what my religion was. Absolutely, nobody cared. The traditional wedding rituals took place in the main temple of the city. Unlike Poland, no one asked me about my religion, and no one in any of the temples pressurised us to declare the religion of our future children.

Anurag's hometown is not very far from the National Capital Region. Relatives and friends arrived from different parts of the country and the world. Everybody just got immersed in the wedding celebration. Post wedding, small kids in the neighbourhood even started to cry when they learnt that their 'Didi' (me) would be living in the National Capital Region and would not be staying as their neighbour in Anurag's parents' home. Those were genuine tears. I was deeply touched.

The birth of 'India In Details'[1]

The global prejudice against Indians and the common media stereotypes of India that I experienced on so many different levels inspired me to do something about changing this adverse viewpoint. As a result, a social media channel – *India in Details*

1 www.indiaindetails.com

was formed. From that point, my career took a completely new turn. It required many personal sacrifices, but I was determined.

Sometimes, it seems that many Westerners, their news outlets and especially the citizens of the former colonial powers, have fully-formed opinions of what an Indian is and what an Indian should be.

This has made the situation pretty delicate in India where a very large population is still suffering from a post-colonial identity crisis and is extremely vulnerable to the biased narratives of the global mainstream media. All of this makes many Indians hate their own identity and cultures. India's living cultural heritage is an asset to the world. Any harm to India's intangible heritage is a harm to our global civilisational heritage. This is a very serious matter. We must realise that India's loss is our loss.

At *India in Details* – Social Media Channel, we have challenged the existing India-hating narratives by taking an academic, analytical and scientific approach.

In no manner do we wish to silence any genuine good-hearted criticism. We encourage the idea of learning the best global practices and we want to participate in the process of finding solutions for the existing problems.

It should also be pointed out that most Indians who I have met (online/offline) are genuinely concerned about finding solutions to their existing problems. And yes, there is absolutely nothing wrong in being self-critical.

However, narratives, which are centered around shaming India without giving the much-required broader perspective, clearly appear to be born out of limited understanding, or seem politically inspired or appear to be driven by some other agenda. Such type of biased and selective journalism should have no place in a healthy society.

Year 2018-19
Does the world perceive India correctly?

India (Bharat) – is an extremely diverse and a complex country. In his book, *A Cultural History of India*, the well-known historian, AL Basham, noted that, 'While there are four main cradles of civilisation which, moving from East to West, are China, India, the Fertile Crescent and the Mediterranean, specially Greece and Italy, India deserves a larger share of credit because she has deeply affected the cultural life of most of Asia. She has also extended her influence, directly and indirectly, to other parts of the world'.

India's unique intangible heritage should be regarded as one of the most fascinating and important parts of our global civilisational heritage. Throughout history, the country has contributed immensely to humankind and even today, there is a lot of hope, promise and solutions that India brings to the global economy, development, peace and well-being.

Even in this digital age, an average Westerner has a very limited understanding of India. Caste, cow and slums are some of the most common words that I hear when I speak to Europeans and Americans about India. In the last couple of years, a new word has entered that list and that is – rape. On various occasions, the global media has even called India the 'rape capital of the world'.

The present India is definitely not a paradise; it is a country that has been trying to rebuild itself after centuries of loot and colonisation. It is a country that has been trying to reclaim its lost position. It is a developing nation, and in various important parameters, it still has a long way to go. However, labelling India as 'the most dangerous country for women' does not only sound inaccurate but also reflects a very reckless and an over-simplified approach in handling such a serious subject.

Sexual crimes against women and children is a global phenomenon. I have dedicated a big part of this book to this subject. A broader – global perspective, which will open more doors to understanding the root cause of such human behaviour, is absolutely required if we are truly serious about fighting this global menace, something that I have tried to achieve in my researches.

A global perspective is also necessary for dealing with subjects like poverty, human behaviour, environment, global warming and climate change. In its attempt to provide a broader perspective, readers, I hope, will say this book does justice to that.

There is no denying that restricting a multi-cultural civilisation like India to 'cow' or 'slums' is an extremely callous, agenda-driven and a propagandic approach. For any rational thinker, it should soon become quite obvious that India cannot be properly understood without opening its multiple, complex layers in a very systematic and careful manner.

ONE

BHARAT (INDIA): A CONTINUOUS CIVILISATION

THERE IS absolutely no denying that the intellectual life of India left its mark throughout the ancient world.

> From the references in indigenous and foreign contemporary literature, it is apparent therefore that India at all times has been famous for its domestic and foreign trade. In Greek history, we find definite mention of the Indian merchants; in the early days of the Roman Empire, India was a great commercial center for the merchants of Italy and Egypt, as it was at a much earlier period for all Asiatic races from Phoenicia in the West to China in the East.
>
> In more than one epoch, the resources of India, natural and industrial, as well as intellectual, have made the wealth of great empires. Its delicate tissues, its marvelous colours and dyes, its porcelains and pottery; its works on metals

> and ivory, its spices and precious stones, its dainty essences and perfumes, have not only been the wonder and delight of Europe, but in no slight degree helped in the revival of its art.[1]

According to Professor HG Rawlinson (an Oxford-trained historian): It is more likely that Pythagoras (BC 570-475) was influenced by India more than by Egypt. Almost all the theories, religions, philosophical and mathematics taught by the Pythagoreans, were known in India in the sixth century BC.... It seems that the so-called Pythagorean theorem of the quadrature of the hypotenuse was already known to the Indians in the older Vedic times, and thus before Pythagoras.[2]

According to Voltaire (a French historian, Enlightenment writer and philosopher, AD 1694-1778), 'The Greek, before the time of Pythagoras, traveled into India for instruction. The signs of the seven planets and of the seven metals are still almost all over the earth, such as the Indians invented: the Arabians were obliged to adopt their cyphers'.[3]

The Japanese scholar Okakura Kakuzō has stated: 'Such a faith in its early energy and enthusiasm was the natural incentive to that great scientific age which was to produce astronomers like Aryabhatta, discovering the revolution of the earth on its own axis; and his not less illustrious successor Varahmihira, who brought Hindu medicine to its height, perhaps under Susruta; and which finally gave to Arabia the knowledge with which she was later to fructify Europe.'[4] With her various common spiritual disciplines

---

1 Source: India as Known to the Ancient World, Dr Gauranganath Banerjee.
2 Legacy of India 1937.
3 The Philosophy of History.
4 Source: The Ideals of the East, with special reference to the Art of Japan.

that connected her diverse population to one another, Bharat with all its Shakti Peethas[5] and many other pilgrimage-centric spiritual landmarks which were scattered all over the subcontinent and beyond, was born long before it was given the name of 'India'.

The knowledge systems of India's civilisational heritage are a global asset. The global community should be encouraged to explore and discover the valuable and relevant elements that it can find from India's literary, linguistic, philosophical, scientific, technological, medical and artistic heritage and from the contributions that the country has made to other civilisations and cultures.

5 Ancient pilgrimage destinations in Shaktism which is a mother goddess-focused Hindu tradition. There are supposed to be 51 such destinations in India.

TWO

21ST CENTURY INDIA

Year 2018-19

INDIA – THE world's largest democracy – is going through a massive transformation.

The 21st century India is responding to globalisation and this is reflected in its transforming cityscapes.

The country has brought 271 million people out of poverty between the years of 2005 to 2016 (UNDP, OPHI).

Standard Chartered's long-term forecast expects India to become the world's second-largest economy by 2030, overtaking the US, and becoming second only to China (January2019).

It should be noted that India has already become the third largest economy in purchasing power terms, and in nominal terms, it is the fifth largest in the world.[1]

According to The Centre for International Development at Harvard University, 'The economic pole of global growth has moved over the past few years from China to neighbouring India, where it is likely to stay over the coming decade'.

In terms of economic progress, is India becoming the next China?

The Beijing based Chinese think-tank, Anbound, thinks so.

According to Anbound, 'China needs to seriously consider and study the rise of India's economy and India's competitive advantage. India, an ancient land with growing young population, is an emerging market power; it is entirely possible for it to become the next China and poses great attraction to the world's capital'.

The Chinese think-tank's apprehensions are not unfounded.

Leading international business leaders, think-tanks and global CEOs now consider India as one of the most attractive destinations for investment and technology transactions.[2]

By 2027, the cumulative wealth of India's population is expected to reach US $25 trillion (India Philanthropy Report 2019). And by then, the country will nearly have a million US dollar millionaires (New World Wealth).

'The high and upper-middle income segment is expected to double from one in four households in 2018 to one in two households by 2030', says the India Philanthropy Report 2019. India already has the second largest telecom network in the world and it is expected to have a total internet user base of more than 800 million by 2021 (829 million by 2021 from 560.01

1 It reached the fifth position, then slipped to the seventh position according to the World Development Indicators issued by The World Bank.

2 EY's 2015 India Attractiveness Survey, E&Y, PwC Global CEO Survey.

million in September 2018, according to Cisco's 13th annual Visual Networking Index-VNI). India has more than 250 million school-going students, which is more than in any other country.

The country has become the second-largest market for e-learning after the US, according to the UK-India Business Council in 2015. A report by Ernst & Young and FICCI (Vision 2030) stated that by 2030, the 'emergence of a robust higher education system would enable India to have more than 20 universities among the global top 200'. In terms of scientific output, India ranks fifth in the world (Scopus) and by 2030, it is expected to climb up to third.

It is expected that by 2034, the Indian e-commerce industry will overtake the US to become the second largest e-commerce market (Worldpay's projections).

In 2017, India ranked first in the Global Retail Development Index.

By 2030 it is set to become the third-largest consumer market (WEF-Bain report).

Connectivity, Infrastructure

The number of operational airports in India will rise to 200 in two decades says the KPMG,FICCI, Vision 2040 for the Civil Aviation Industry in India and by 2024, it will overtake the UK to become the third-largest air passenger market, predicts IATA. That is just four years from now.

Ports, rail, highways… ambitious infrastructure projects are rapidly changing the face of India. The country is already building its bullet train infrastructure and it is also working on the Hyperloop. India's state-of-the-art Train 18 (Vande Bharat Express), which is a semi-high speed indigenously built train has already found many global admirers who have expressed an interest in importing it.

India is already creating a web of modern urban metro networks in its big cities. After the completion of phase 4, the Delhi metro will become the third largest metro network in the world with a total length of approximately 450 km (DMRC).

With more than 7,000 freight trains carrying 3 million tonnes of freight daily and more than 12,000 passenger trains with 23 million travelers on board every day, the Indian Railways, with its 115,000 km network and more than 7,000 stations is among the world's largest (Government of India).

Spanning over 5.5 million km, India has the world's second largest road network, and by 2022 the country is expected to have a national highway network of 200,000 km (NHAI).

India is not just planning to be well connected internally but it is also working on projects that will make it better connected with the rest of the world.

Apart from developing Sittwe Port in Myanmar and Chabahar port in Iran, India has joined the Ashqabat agreement which will diversify India's connectivity options with Central Asia. This agreement is expected to synchronise with India's efforts to implement the International North-South Transport Corridor (INSTC) for improved connectivity with Eurasia.

New Delhi is also focused on the completion of the India-Myanmar-Thailand Trilateral Highway and there is already a plan to extend this highway to Cambodia, Laos and Vietnam.

India is also assisting other nations by extending loans worth billions of dollars.

It has 279 LOCs (Lines of Credit) which are worth $ 28 billion in 63 nations in Africa, Asia, Latin America, Caribbean and Oceania. 'Of this, 254 projects aggregating nearly $4.70 billion have been completed, while 194 projects worth nearly $19 billion are under implementation. These include 94 connectivity projects in five countries in India's immediate neighbourhood being taken up with LOC worth nearly $6.6 billion (V Muraleedharan, June 2019, in Parliament of India).

India is developing or planning five industrial corridors that are supposed to be the core elements in India's growth story.

India is expected to have 30.5 million international (annually) tourist arrivals by 2028, but its real potential is a lot more, says the government.

With 26 biotic provinces, 10 bio-geographical zones, more than 30 World Heritage sites, a 7000 km coastal line, as well as its mountains, deserts, rainforests, islands, volcano, salt flats, wildlife, and tribal habitation – India is incredibly diversified.

Its 28 states, nine union territories, 4,000 cities and 600,000 villages have a lot of hidden potential; many of them are not yet fully explored and discovered.

In 2017, India ranked first in the world's first Digital Traveler Rankings when it was revealed that it had the most digitally advanced travellers (Travelport). India is also emerging as a lucrative expat destination.

It is the 12th best country to live in as an expat. It is far ahead of countries like the USA (23rd), the UK (22nd), Japan (30th) and China (27th), says the HSBC's Expat Explorer Survey 2018. India-based expats earn an average of USD 176,408, which means that they are the second-highest paid in the world (HSBC's Expat Explorer Survey 2017). On the other hand, Indians who are living outside India have performed exceptionally well and have rightfully earned the tag of 'model minority'. In both the UK and the USA, the Indian community has been outperforming other ethnic groups academically and economically, says the PEW Research Center, Race Disparity Audit, 2017. India is also the world's top recipient of remittances as its diaspora sent USD 79 billion back home in 2018, says the World Bank. The country is also expected to benefit from the reverse brain drain.

Overseas Indians

UAE, UK, USA or Kenya, the Indian community has contributed immensely to their adopted country whether it is education, medicine, philanthropy or economics. Whether the presented circumstances were favourable or adverse in the adopted nations, the Indian community has largely excelled.

United States of America

Globally, there are more than 30 million overseas Indians. Overseas Indians include nonresident Indians (NRI) and persons of Indian origin (PIO). Just in the US, the population of overseas Indians is around 4.5 million out of which around 3.2 million are PIOs and 1. 3 million are NRIs, says India's Ministry of External Affairs.

Overseas Indians who are living in the US are playing a massive role in the country's economy.

In 2005, the US Congress passed House Resolution 227 which praised the stellar work done by Indian Americans in all walks of life. It also urged 'all Americans to recognise the contributions of Indian Americans and have a greater appreciation of the role they have played in helping to advance and enrich American society'.[3] In 2003, the investment firm Merrill Lynch estimated there were 200,000 millionaires of Indian origin. That was more than fifteen

---

3 Congress.gov, H Res.227 – 109th Congress (2005-2006).

years ago; in times when the population of overseas Indians was far lesser than what it is today. The number of the millionaires of Indian origin should be a lot higher today.

The 2010 census of USINPAC stated that in the USA, 223,000 Indian-owned firms employ more than 600,000 employees.

According to a 2014 study, 15 per cent of startups in Silicon Valley were founded by Indians even though Indians made up just 6 per cent of the Valley's working population and what is even more astonishing is that Indians alone founded more start-ups than the next four communities combined who were from China, Japan, Britain and Taiwan.[4]

According to Safra Catz, the CEO of the Software major Oracle corporation, 75 per cent of its management is from India (an exclusive interview with TOI, 2016).

Pepsi, Microsoft, MasterCard, Google, Adobe, SanDisk, all of them have had CEOs who have at least finished their graduation (bachelors) from India.

India is the top supplier of doctors to the USA (International Migration Outlook 2015, OECD).

Not only that, according to National Foundation for American Policy, among all immigrants, India was the leading country of origin with 14 founders of billion-dollar companies.

Very interestingly, among 29 million scientists and engineers in the US, almost 1 million are Indian, more than any other country in the world, even more than the entire Europe (National Science Foundation, National Center for Science and Engineering Statistics, SESTAT).

---

4 Vivek Wadhwa (Director of Research at the Center for Entrepreneurship and Research Commercialisation at the Pratt School of Engineering, Duke University).

Not just that, nearly half of the motels in the US are owned by Indians and a vast majority of them are owned by the Patels of Gujarat.[5]

From owning and operating full-service hotels like Marriott, Sheraton and Hilton to properties like Holiday Inns, Comfort Inns, Quality Inns, AAHOA members have done very well in the American hotel industry. According to the author Joel Millman, 'Patels took a sleepy, mature industry and turned it upside down offering consumers more choices while making the properties themselves more profitable. Motels that attracted billions in immigrant savings turned into real estate equity worth many billions more' (*The Other Americans* by Joel Millman).The 2018 report by the US-based National Association of Realtors (NAR) revealed that India is among the top five countries of origin for homebuyers in the US. Indian Americans are the richest ethnic communities in the US with a median household income of 114,261 USD.[6]

Socioeconomically, Indian Americans lead every other ethnic group in the US. Hindus are the most educated religious community in the USA. Seventyone per cent of all Indians have a bachelor's degree or higher and in comparison, the national average is just 28 per cent while 44 per cent is the average of all Asian American groups. As many as 40 per cent of all Indians in the United States have a doctorate, master's degree or other professional degree which is again five times the national average.

---

5 Yudhijit Bhattacharjee, National Geographic, 2018, https://www.nationalgeographic.com/culture/2018/09/south-asia-america-motels-immigration/

6 Income in the past 12 months (In 2017 Inflation Adjusted Dollars), US Census Bureau 2017, Retrieved18. 7.19.

Not just that, there are thousands of Indian-Americans who serve as faculties in the universities across the US.

Multiple researches have indicated that parental divorce and a poor family structure have strong impacts on children's educational attainment. A strong family bond is very important for Indians.

In terms of family structure, Indian Americans are 'more likely to be currently married than US adults overall and to have lower rates of birth outside of marriage'; 71 per cent of adult Indian Americans are married, a per centage much higher than the rest of the Americans who now mostly live a single life. The share of unmarried mothers is just around 2.3 per cent in Indian Americans while the nation's average is 37 per cent (2012 PEW Research, based on 2010 ACS).

Yes, better education and stable families are directly connected with wealth. Indian values are now enriching 21st century America.

Sewa and philanthropy by Indian Americans

'Forty million people struggle with hunger in the United States, including more than 12 million children', says Feeding America.

In 2017, 39.7 million people (in the USA) were living in poverty, according to the US Census Bureau. 'On a single night in 2018, roughly 553,000 people were experiencing homelessness in the United States'/ and one-fifth of them were children (20 per cent or 111,592). 'African Americans account for 40 per cent of all people experiencing Homelessness' and '6 in 10 people experiencing unsheltered homelessness (most of whom do so as individuals) are white.'[7]

---

7 The US Department of Housing and Urban Development, The 2018 Annual Homeless Assessment Report.

The Indian American community, which is the richest ethnic group in the USA, also understands its social responsibility.

In Indian parlance, this philanthropic act is called *seva* (or sewa) which literally means 'selfless service'. 'Seva bhav' has no ulterior motives. The traditional Dharmic Indian system encourages universal familyhood and sees divinity in everything that exists.

Many Indian Americans have enthusiastically participated in various types of philanthropic work. It is not just the Gurudwaras and temples that distribute free meals and provide basic amenities, many Indian Americans and non-profit organisations also work day and night to uplift the lives of various under-served individuals and communities.

Fighting the non-friendly side

The discrimination and bullying of Hindus in the United States underlines a very serious issue. In 2016, HAF's report highlighted the unsettling experiences that many Hindu students in America face on a frequent basis. That year, one out of three students had reported that they were bullied for their religious beliefs.

One in eight students reported that their teachers made sarcastic remarks about Hinduism in front of a class.

Half of the students surveyed felt socially alienated due to their religion.

Though the survey was limited due to its sample size of about 350, it did manage to reveal the scale of religious bullying that many Hindu students in America are subjected to, and was suggestive enough to raise serious questions for 'more in-depth testing'.

Multiple studies have indicated that bullying is linked to many negative outcomes and can leave lifelong scars.

Unfortunately, overall general bullying is nothing new in American schools.

'During 2017, 19.0 per cent of high school students nationwide were bullied on school property during the 12 months before the survey', says the Youth Risk Behavior Surveillance, United States, 2017, CDC. In a progressive society, it is important to stand against discrimination and injustice. It is also important to empower those who are at the risk of being mentally or civilsationally displaced.

United States desires to be a country where people of all backgrounds, all languages, and all religions can make a home.

To achieve that, it must create conditions in which individuals can develop a sense of security and self-worth.

H1B issues

It is well documented that Indian scientists and engineers fill the American skill deficit and contribute to the American economy. Not only that, many high-skilled Indians establish new businesses, which also lead to the creation of many new jobs in America. Numerous studies have shown that there are not enough numbers of skilled Americans for the jobs that many Indian IT companies are creating in the United States.

The H1- B visa programme helps the companies in the USA by letting them hire highly skilled foreign professionals in areas where there is a shortage of qualified American workers.

According to a report that was published in 2015, IT Talent Shortage is the biggest problem that the US technology economy is facing. (Source: *Service Providers are Waging War Against US Talent Shortage With Unconventional Methods*, Allie Young, Helen Huntley).

According to the US Department of Labour, there are going to be 1.4 million computer specialist job openings in the USA by 2020, but universities are unlikely to deliver even 30 per cent of the numbers of skilled graduates that are required.

The 2016 state of the CIO survey revealed 49 per cent of CIOs were expecting shortages in IT professionals in the next one year.

Indian IT companies, which are operating in the USA, sensed this shortage in skilled professionals and that is why they have been assisting American universities by backing STEM (Science, Technology, Engineering, and Math) education programmes.

Since 2009, an Indian tech giant TCS has been running a free flagship community-engagement programme called goIT, which has provided more than 100,000 hours of 'high-impact skill building' for students in North America. According to TCS, more than 10,000 North American students have engaged in this programme in 32 cities and the students also include girls, minorities and underserved groups.

Another Indian company Infosys is also trying to counter this deficit of IT workers in the USA. It has provided training to 2,500 teachers and 135,000 students through its education programmes and it is also funding the training of 1,000 public school teachers in Computer Science (Source: Infosys). In the last few years, Infosys Foundation USA has made multiple investments to bridge the digital divide in America by supporting high quality computer science education and coding skills.

Wipro, which is Bengaluru-based, is also funding the training of hundreds of teachers by partnering with universities in different places (Michigan, Boston, Texas) of the US (Source: Wipro).

TCS is among the top two job creators in the American IT

services sector. According to a study by The Cambridge Group, from 2012 to 2016, TCS recruited more than 12,500 workers from the US and emerged as a top employer of American talent.

Globally, TCS employs more than 387,000 consultants in 45 countries and in the US, it recruits from over 75 US college campuses (TCS).

Other Indian companies are doing something similar. In 2017, Infosys announced that it plans to hire 10,000 American workers over the next two years.

Since the USA suffers from an IT talent shortage, the role of highly skilled foreign professionals has become extremely crucial to fill that gap and many IT workers from India who hold the H1-B visa are doing exactly that.

Moreover, many Indian immigrants end up establishing their own companies in the US and that creates even more jobs and trade opportunities for US born workers.

Moreover, the Hunt study (2011) showed that in the USA, two per cent of immigrants, compared to 0.9 per cent of natives had been granted a patent in the previous 5 years. It also showed that immigrants were ahead of natives in licensing or commercialising patents (1.3 per cent of immigrants compared to 0.6 per cent of natives).

Other studies have shown that a lot of applicants who filed patents in the US had Indian names.[8] Hundreds of thousands of skilled workers from India are the backbone of American STEM industries, especially when IT talent Shortage is the biggest problem that the US technology economy is facing.

---

8 The Agglomeration of US Ethnic Inventors by William R Kerr, The Supply Side of Innovation: H-1B Visa Reforms and US Ethnic Invention, William R Kerr, William F Lincoln.

If the US Government's policies become less friendly for Indian workers, it could cause brain drain in the US and could even encourage the American companies to further offshore jobs.

And anyway, someone's loss is someone else's gain.

Is it possible that America's brain drain can be India's brain gain? A report by AeA, The Losing the Competitive Advantage Report, which was released by a high-tech lobbying group in the US, had already talked about this a few years ago (AeA later merged with Information Technology Association of America (ITAA) to form TechAmerica).

Reform may be needed in the H-1B visa system to make it fairer so that it is not misused.

But what Indians have brought to the land of the United States is very well known. They have brought knowledge and innovation, they have brought their spiritual wealth and their unique heritage, they have brought big investments and they have also created jobs.

United Kingdom

While British Indians are barely two per cent of the UK's population, they are 12 per cent of all doctors (General Medical Council, UK).

Indian doctors are viewed as the backbone of Britain's National Health Service. India is the top supplier of doctors to the UK (International Migration Outlook 2015, OECD) and the NHS has always turned to India to address its staff shortages, but, unfortunately, its racist practices towards Indian doctors have not stopped. And this not only applies to doctors, the NHS has also turned to India for 'generic' versions of branded drugs. And thanks to the medicines that are manufactured in India, Britain's

NHS has saved billions of pounds.

For India's pharmaceuticals exports, the UK is the second largest market (PHARMEXCIL).

India's role in lowering healthcare costs in the UK is crucial as the UK has a growing number of elderly people. The number of people living with diabetes in the UK is rapidly increasing and according to Barbara Young of Diabetes UK, Diabetes may even bankrupt the NHS.

It is not just the NHS, which has regularly turned to India to seek doctors and medicines for ailing UK citizens. According to the International Passenger Survey, Office for National Statistics, the number of people going to India for healthcare has also been increasing. Between 2015 and 2016, the number of UK visitors for medical treatment in India increased by 242 per centum. Britain's NHS is facing a major crisis as there are not enough beds, doctors and nurses and there is not enough money.

In 2018, 500,000 patients were waiting more than 18 weeks to start planned treatment – the highest in almost a decade (NHS 'referral to treatment' RTT statistics for April 2018).

The conditions are no less frightening in Northern Ireland, where more than 80,000 patients have waited more than a year for their first appointment with a consultant (by December 31, 2017; UK Department of Health).

It is no surprise that the number of people going abroad for healthcare is constantly rising.

The total departures from the UK for medical treatment has dramatically risen from 48,000 in 2014 to almost 144,000 in 2016 (International Passenger Survey, Office for National Statistics).

According to Kings Fund, institutional racism is a major problem in the NHS. The career path for non-White staff is frequently obstructed and that is the reason why there are not many Indian doctors in very senior positions, even though they are highly talented.

In 2018, a study, commissioned by Sky to mark National Inclusion Week revealed that more than a quarter of British workers experienced discrimination in the workplace.

At 82 per cent, race is the main motivation behind hate crimes in England and Wales. If you are Black, you are more than twice as likely to be murdered (Equality and Human Rights Commission, 2016).

Discrimination and hate crimes are nothing new in Britain.

In 1863, James Hunt, the President of the London Anthropological Society, wrote in his paper, 'the Negro is inferior intellectually to the European... (and) can only be humanised and civilised by Europeans' (On the Negro's Place in Nature).

The seeds of racism are deeply rooted and many members of the society continue to feel superior to non-whites. During my interaction with many British Indians, I discovered that many of them regularly face racism and discrimination and have chosen to accept this as a part of their lives. The conditions may not be very fair, but British Indians have remained focused and committed.

Actually, their focus and commitment start at school.

In terms of the grades secured in schools, Indian students perform better than the national average and they also outperform white British students.

A two-year research project (2013-2015) revealed that Indians students consistently achieved better results than white British students throughout the whole period (1993-2013).[9]

Not just that, Indian students are also more likely to go on to a top-flight university.

Shining bright in adverse conditions

Yes, ethnic minorities are indeed massively underrepresented in the UK in positions of power and authority (Equality and Human Rights Commission, 2016).

Yes, it is true that the Indian community has found it difficult to get public sector jobs even though they are known for their high grades and talent.

Yes, it is true that even highly-skilled Indian doctors find many obstructions in their career path in the NHS due to racism and discrimination.

But this hasn't stopped British Indians from becoming successful.

Perhaps, the secret behind their success stories is the fact that they have really learned how to perform in adverse conditions.

That is why every third Indian household in the UK earns over 1,000 GBP each week which puts them into the wealthiest category (Race Disparity Audit, 2017).

That is why British Indians are hardly two per cent of the UK's population but they contribute six per cent of the country's GDP, says Ministry of External Affairs, India

That is why, among all ethnicities, Indians are the most likely to work in the highest-skilled occupational groups. Over one in 10 are

9 Race, Racism and Education: Inequality, resilience and reform in policy & practice, David Gillborn, Nicola Rollock, Paul Warmington, Sean Demack.

in Director, Manager and Senior Official roles and more than three in 10 are in Professional occupations (Race Disparity Audit, 2017).

British Indians have performed exceptionally well in a nation that is known for its centuries-old tradition of racism and discrimination. If the UK can create an atmosphere that is free from racism, British Indians are more than ready to play an even bigger role in helping the country that is looking to find its way after leaving the European Union.

United Arab Emirates

Over the last three decades, the Indian community has played a significant role in the economic development of the United Arab Emirates.

The population of the UAE is around 9.2 million out of which only 1.4 million are Emirati citizens and 7.8 million are expatriates, according to one United Nations estimate.

The UAE is home to an Indian expatriate community of more than 2.8 million (MEA, Govt of India).

From these 2.8 million Indians, 15 per cent are professionals and businessmen and their family members; 20 per cent are white-collar nonprofessionals (shop assistants, salesman, accountants, clerical staff etc.) and the remaining 65 per cent are blue-collar workers who are mostly employed in agriculture farms, construction companies and municipalities (Embassy of India in the UAE).

According to the 2005 report by Merrill Lynch, around 33,000 Indian millionaires were living in the UAE.

The Indian companies have emerged as important investors in the free trade zones of the UAE such as Hamariya free zone, Sharjah Airport, Abu Dhabi industrial city and the Jebel Ali Free Zone Area.

Just in the Jebel Ali Free zone Area (JAFZA), there are more than 800 leading Indian companies.[10]

There is a long list of successful dollar billionaires and millionaires in the UAE that comes from the Indian community among them personalities like Yussuf Ali, Dr BR Shetty and Sunny Varkey have received Padma Shree, which is the fourth highest civilian award in the Republic of India.

Indians are also playing a crucial role in the UAE in the field of higher education, as the Gulf Medical University with its campus in Ajman is founded by Thumbay Moideen and is very well-known, with students from all over the world.

In 2015, the annual remittance made by the Indian community in the UAE was around 12.5 billion USD and it was highest among all other nationalities (PEW research center).

Most Indians live in the three largest cities of the UAE – Dubai, Sharjah and Abu Dhabi and a lot of them are from Kerala and Tamil Nadu. It is important to point out that in the UAE, citizenship and naturalisation is extremely hard and even if you are a citizen, your citizenship can be taken away for a variety of reasons. This explains why the number of PIOs in the UAE is just 3,751, even though the UAE has the fourth-largest population of overseas Indians in the world (Government of India, 2016). In terms of NRIs, the UAE is the second highest, with only Saudi Arabia ahead of it. As a matter of fact, a low number of PIOs and a high number of NRIs are common in Gulf countries.

Not many people know that even after the independence of India, the Indian Rupee continued to be the official currency in

---

10 http://jafza.ae/news/jafza-reports-10-growth-in-the-number-of-indian-companies/ retrieved on 17-6-19.

the UAE, long before the UAE dirham even existed. In 1957, special notes, which were known as 'Gulf Rupees' or 'External Rupees' were printed in India, and these stayed in circulation in the UAE until 1966 when India devalued its currency and by that time, oil had been discovered in the Gulf.

India's industrial scenario

India is the number-one offshoring destination in the world, accounting for approximately 55 per cent market share of the (US$ 185-190 billion) global services sourcing business (in 2017-18, NASSCOM 2018).

Indian IT (and ITeS) companies have a presence in more than 80 countries and Indian IT giant TCS is set to become world's third-largest IT services company.

India has the world's third-largest startup ecosystem (Nasscom-start-up-report-2017). India is the second largest casting producer in the world (World Casting Census 2016).

It is also the second largest producer of steel and cement (World Steel Association, Global Cement Directory 2018).

The construction market in India will grow nearly twice as fast as China up to 2030 and the country is expected to overtake Japan to become world's third largest construction market by 2021 (Source: Global Construction 2030).

Thanks to that, there shouldn't be any surprise that the Indian real estate industry is expected to be the third largest in the world by 2030 (KPMG-Naredco-APREA, 2018).

India is already the second largest mobile phone manufacturer (120 factories) in the world, says the Indian Cellular Association, giving the data of July 2018. Mobile usage and production can only grow with a young population.

It is (in FY18) the third largest producer of coal and fourth largest producer of iron ore, says Government of India's data.

The country is the world's largest cutting and polishing center for diamonds, and in 2017, it exported 75 per cent of the world's polished diamonds (Gems and Jewellery Export Promotion Council, GJEPC).

By 2020, it is expected to become the fifth largest manufacturing country in the world, according to the Global Manufacturing Competitiveness Index published by Deloitte.

In 2017, India became the fourth largest auto market.

It is already the largest manufacturer of two-wheelers and tractors in the world. It is the world's third-largest heavy truck manufacturer and fourth-largest car producer (Government data). By 2020, it is expected to become the fourth-largest manufacturer of automobiles globally, after China, the US and Japan (Grant Thornton – Making Indian Auto Component Industry Future-Ready, Feb 2018) and the Indian auto-components industry is set to become the third-largest in the world by 2025, says the government. Jaguar, Land Rover / Range Rover, and SangYong Motors are owned by Indian companies.

A healthcare giant

India's national healthcare programme, Ayushman Bharat, is the largest government-funded healthcare programme in the world (Govt of India). The country also contributes immensely to global healthcare. India is the top supplier of doctors to both the UK and the USA (International Migration Outlook 2015, OECD).

Indian hospitals receive nearly 500,000 international patients annually and medical tourism in the country is expected to touch USD 8 billion by 2020 (Govt figures, 2017, Grant Thornton).

It is difficult to imagine how the world would be able to combat AIDS without Indian input.

Globally, over 80 per cent of the antiretroviral drugs which are used to combat AIDS are supplied by Government of India. India produces lifesaving drugs that includes the likes of generic anti-AIDS medicine Tenofovir Alafenamide (TAF), which are saving many lives in 112 developing countries (GoI).

India supplies thirty per cent of the annual UNICEF requirement of anti-retroviral drugs.[11]

Indian drugs are exported to more than nearly 200 countries in the world. Since India is the largest provider of generic drugs globally, it is also known as 'the pharmacy of the world'.

Twentyfive per cent of all medicines in the UK are sourced from India; 40 per cent of generic drugs taken by Americans are made in India, and the county's massive pharmaceutical industry is the source of more than 50 per cent of global demand for various vaccines (Pharmexcil / Govt of India).

Agriculture

India's rich culture and spiritual foundation wisdom are its big assets. It is the land which gave birth to pro-environment traditions like 'Aparigraha'. The Dharmic tradition, Aparigraha, is about non-possessivenes and self-discipline which means taking only what is absolutely necessary.

The Indian State of Sikkim has become the role model for the entire world in organic farming. It is the world's first 100 per cent organic state (FAO).

---

11 Quality Excellence: The next frontier for Indian pharma industry, IPA white paper, 2016.

India has the highest number of organic producers in the world and is home to 30 per centof total organic producers globally, says the World of Organic Agriculture 2018 report.

Fruit and vegetable production, tea production, silk production, bamboo genetic resources – India ranks second in the world in all these departments.[12] In other agricultural commodities like rice, wheat and pulses it is also among the top producers (APEDA).

With as many as 8,000 species, India is the world's second largest exporter of medicinal plants, says the Botanical Survey of India (BSI), India's Ministry of Environment, Forests & Climate Change.

It is the world's largest producer of dairy and spices, and globally, India has been the largest milk-producing country since 1997 (APEDA, A Study of India's Dairy Sector 2017).

After the United States, Japan and China, India is the fourth-largest producer of agrochemicals (FICCI).

A promising future

Some of the biggest solar farms of the world are located in India. The Indian renewable energy sector is the fourth-most-attractive renewable energy market in the world, says the Renewable Energy Country Attractiveness index 2018 by EY and the country is well-positioned to surpass its 2022 renewable energy target (175 GW).

In Paris, India pledged that by 2030, 40 per cent of its installed energy production capacity will come from renewable sources and it is expected that by 2050, renewables will supply 75 per cent of electricity in India (New Energy Outlook (NEO) 2018).

12 Source: APEDA, India, FAO; Central Silk Board (Ministry of Textiles, Govt of India): FAO report, World Forest Resources.

Thorium is considered to be the 'nuclear fuel of the future' and India has one of the largest shares of global thorium reserves, says the Govt of India.

From its film industry to its space agency and defense, India's growth can be seen across a very broad spectrum.

In terms of ticket sales and number of films made, India has the world's largest film industry, says the government.

India is a nuclear armed nation, and its military is the fourth strongest in the world, reports Global Firepower, 2018.

Its space agency, ISRO, has already reached Mars and now it is planning to have its own space station. It is also planning to send humans to space. Through its commercial arm, Antrix, it has launched hundreds of foreign satellites for multiple developed and developing nations (ISRO).

This may all sound very impressive but for India, this is just the beginning. It wants to attain self-dependence in core technologies, and it wants to participate in the Fourth Industrial Revolution.

But will India be able to earn its rightful place in the powerful and influential global forums which are dominated by the western nations?

Will India be able to help those forums become truly global and truly democratic by challenging the existing supremacy of the western powers?

Will India be able to protect its citizens from tech-colonisation, and will it be able to have a stronger voice in the global media?

Will India be able to protect its identity from the western religious and commercial monocultures which are homogenising its cultures and diversity? Will it be able to learn the best global practices and will it able to preserve the best that it has?

Unlike others, will India be able to use its science for global public good and not just for commercial returns?

Those who are concerned about India's economic development's impact on the environment, should also understand that India's historical (cumulative) emissions are extremely low in comparison to other global powers, as the World Resources Institute points out.

Just because the financial prosperity of many developed nations and colonial powers came at a cost to the environment and through the misery of colonised nations, it does not mean that there are no other ways to walk the path to prosperity.

Through its approach of universal familyhood which is rooted in its ancient foundational wisdom, India is practicing what others could only preach.

The world should take note of that.

THREE

IS INDIA ONLY ABOUT HINDI AND HINDUS?

IN THE European Parliament, on the occasion of the Golden Jubilee year of the European Union, the former president of India APJ Abdul Kalam, said, 'I am reminded of the dream of the Indian poet Kaniyan Poongkundranaar, who 3,000 years ago, said in the Tamil Classic *Purananuru* "Yaadhum Oorae Yaavarum Kaeleer", which means 'I am a world citizen, every citizen is my own kith and kin"'. Abdul Kalam – an aerospace scientist, who served as the 11th President of India – was adored and admired by people from all backgrounds and age groups. A vast majority of the Indian population has Dharmic[1] roots. Not all Indians

1 A life centered around karma, reincarnation and yoga.

are Hindus, but it should be pointed out that a vast majority of Hindus who live on our planet are in India.

India is the birthplace of all Dharmic traditions, and the people of India have even accommodated the ideologies and religions that were born elsewhere. Hindus form the majority in the country, and Hindi is spoken by a very large population, but India is not just about Hindi and Hindus.[2]

India has a variety of religions and languages. Apart from religions like Islam and Christianity, there are also many people in India who follow Zoroastrianism, Judaism and the Baha'i faith. Other lesser-known religions like Bathouism, Sarnaism, Sanamahism, Donyi-Polo and the animist religion of Santhals, Gonds and other tribal people are also practised in India.

India has 22 official languages, and English is an additional official language. Languages like Portuguese and French are also spoken among some people in India, especially in those parts which were former colonies of France and Portugal. But the actual language diversity of India is much greater. According to the People's Linguistic Survey of India (PLSI), India has over 780 languages and 66 different scripts and researchers believe that there are at least one hundred more languages that couldn't be reported in the survey. Arunachal Pradesh alone has 90 languages, and West Bengal has the highest number of scripts among all States, totaling nine. Assam, with 55 languages, Gujarat with 48, and Maharashtra with 39 are some of the most linguistically diverse states of India. However, in the 2001 Census of India, in which a different calculation method was used, it was reported

2 Source: Census, 2011, India.

that there are 1599 other languages and 122 major languages.

As far as Sanskrit is concerned, it is still spoken in a few villages of India, including Jhiri of Madhya Pradesh, Hoshalli and Mattur of Karnataka and Sasana of Odisha. Sanskrit has a strong influence on many Indian languages. It is worth noting that regardless of the regional language of the area, Sanskrit continues to be widely used in everyday prayers, wedding ceremonies, cremation ceremonies, and many other important Hindu religious events across India.

However, all is not well with India's languages. Many of them are just dying. It is estimated that around 220 languages have disappeared in the last 50 years, and another 150 could become extinct in the next five decades. As a nation, India is blessed to have a very rich cultural heritage, but will it able to preserve its identity in the coming decades? The world has many Islamic nations, Christian nations, secular nations, Buddhist nations, a Jewish nation but there is no Hindu nation.

One has plenty of examples if one wants to study how Islamic, Christian or Buddhist nations function but no example of how a Hindu nation functions. For a researcher who would like to study or compare the administrative qualities and functioning of countries with a different religious orientation, the absence of a Hindu nation can be a frustrating blockade.

Nations with a particular religious identity also act as dedicated sanctuaries for those religions so that their religious traditions and ethos can be preserved without any opposition from others. With multiple Islamic and Christian nations in our world, it can be believed that both Abrahamic religions and their traditions are well-preserved and well-guarded.

A recent report, which was produced by the PEW research center, revealed that globally, there are more than 80 countries that directly or indirectly favour specific religions and India is not on that list.

However, many countries in Europe officially or unofficially favour Christianity and that even includes some well-known names like the United Kingdom, Spain, Italy, Greece, Denmark, Finland, Norway and Iceland. The report discovered that countries offer benefits to their preferred religions by giving financial, legal or other practical benefits.

The report also reveals that there is no country in the world that officially or unofficially, favours Hinduism.

Questions should be asked to those nations which clearly favour a particular religion over others by giving them financial, legal or other practical benefits and act as the global role models by preaching equality, freedom and secularism.

The report also reveals that there is no country in the world that names Hinduism as its official state religion, even though it is well known that Hinduism is followed by more than a billion people globally. On the other hand, there are 43 countries in the world which clearly have a state religion and there are many such countries in Europe as well.

Is yoga Hindu?

Can we separate Hinduism from OM (AUM)? Can we separate OM (AUM) from Sanatan Dharma? Can we separate Sanatan Dharma from Karma or can we separate Karma from reincarnation? Can we separate reincarnation from the journey that leads to experiencing union? And can we talk about experiencing union and not talk about Yoga?

No, we can't because Yoga means experiencing union.

Yoga cannot be separated from reincarnation and karma – primarily because these are the two foundational elements of

Sanatan Dharma and India's Dharmic traditions.

So, there is no denying that Yoga has its roots in Hinduism, and it is part of India's rich intangible cultural heritage and its Dharmic knowledge traditions.

Regardless of the beneficiary's religion or nationality, Yoga can help anyone who wants to genuinely experience tranquility, the same tranquility which is the essence of Sanatan Dharma.

The earliest mention of Yoga can be found in Rig Veda and Patanjali is considered as the father of Yoga.

The four paths of Yoga are:

1 Bhakti Yoga: It is the path of devotional bliss.
2 Karma Yoga: It is the path of action. Every action carries an intention and its ethical value.
3 Gyan (Jnana) Yoga: The philosophical path to gain knowledge through reasoning, questioning, study, experience and practice.
4 Raja Yoga or Ashtanga Yoga which is further classified into eight steps:
    a) Yama (restraints)
    b) Niyama (observances)
    c) Asana (physical postures)
    d) Pranayama (controlled breathing)
    e) Pratyahara (withdrawal of the senses)
    f) Dharana (concentration of the mind)
    g) Dhyana (meditation)
    h) Samadhi (absorption)

From the above list, I have experienced that an average Westerner's understanding of yoga is generally limited to 4 (c), 4 (d) and to some extent 4 (g).

Yoga, a personal and a spiritual experience, transformed into a global commercial industry as soon as the West got interested in it. There are more practitioners of Yoga in India than anywhere else in the world, but the US has the biggest chunk of 27 billion USD out of the 80 billion USD global yoga industry.[3] In the USA, more than $16 billion was spent on yoga clothing, equipment, classes and accessories in 2015.[4]

A 2016 survey reported, '34 per cent of Americans say they are somewhat or very likely to practice yoga in the next 12 months – equal to more than 80 million Americans. Reasons cited include flexibility, stress relief and fitness'.[5]

The survey also found that yoga practitioners are more likely to have 'a good sense of balance' and are keener to 'give back to community'. They also become 'highly concerned about their health and the environment'. Half of practitioners 'live green and eat sustainably'.

In Australia, a 2016 research found that one in 10 Australians aged 14 and over do yoga and has become far more popular than aerobics.[6]

Yoga's growing popularity in the West has also opened the floodgates for those who are driven by greed, deceit and commercial interests.

In the West, there are sections which have tried to make yoga their own patented property[7], there are sections which have even

3 How Yoga Became A $27 Billion Industry-And Reinvented American Spirituality | Huff Post India.
4 The 2016 Yoga in America Study-Conducted by Yoga Journal and Yoga Alliance.
5 The 2016 Yoga in America Study-Conducted by Yoga Journal and Yoga Alliance.
6 Roy Morgan Research, 2016.
7 A study conducted by Brain League IP Services, Bangalore.

tried to rename ancient Indian Yoga techniques (eg: Anulom Vilom Pranayama as cardiac coherence breathing),[8] there are sections which have launched weird sounding things like beer yoga[9] and goat yoga;[10] there are sections which have even tried to Christianise yoga;[11] and then finally there are sections which have called Hinduism 'demonic', meditation 'spiritually dangerous' and yoga poses as something which 'were created with demonic intent', to open you up to demonic power.[12] India's yoga has now reached American hands.

Are you brainwashed about Hindus?

By spreading knowledge, we can combat those who spread hate.

But can we also make it work for Hindus who frequently face various forms of insults and abuse?

Demonic, devil worshipers, animal worshipers, dotheads, cow urine / pee drinkers...there is a lot of abuse and hatred that an average Hindu faces on a regular basis.

What is the source of such insults? Is it the hatred in their hearts that some people hold for them? Or is it the overall limited understanding of the global community regarding Hindus, Hinduism and Sanatan Dharm?

In America, despite their immense contribution to wealth generation and philanthropy, and despite being the most educated

8 Proper Breathing Brings Better Health, By Christophe André on January 15, 2019, Scientific American.

9 Beer yoga is popping up all over the world, combining asanas and alcohol, Annemarie McCarthy, Lonely Planet 1 Writer.

10 'Goat yoga' is a thing - and hundreds are lining up for it, By AJ Willingham, CNN.

11 https://holyyoga.net/

12 Missouri Megachurch Pastor Condemns Yoga, Calls Hinduism 'Demonic', Katherine Hignett on 11/13/18, Newsweek.

religious group, Hindus are not regarded as warmly as Catholics, Jewish people and Evangelical Christians (PEW Research Center).

Why?

On occasions, even Hindu temples in America have been vandalised, and in the 1980s and 1990s, they were openly attacked in New Jersey by an American hate group, 'the Dotbusters'.[13]

Within India and abroad, from Winston Churchill and Charles Dickens to recent incidents, the trend of vilifying, mocking, or hurting Hindus appears to be quite old and systematic in nature.

> I hate Indians. They are a beastly people with a beastly religion.
>
> —**Winston Churchill**, Former Prime Minister, Great Britain.

> The PM (Winston Churchill) said the Hindus were a foul race 'protected by their mere pullulation from the doom that is their due' and he wished Bert Harris could send some of his surplus bombers to destroy them.
>
> —**John Colville**'s, diary entry of 23 February 1945.

> I, The Inimitable, holding this office of mine, and firmly believing that I hold it by the permission of Heaven and not by the appointment of Satan, have the honor to inform you Hindoo gentry that it is my intention, with all possible avoidance of unnecessary cruelty and with all merciful swiftness of execution, to exterminate the Race from the face of the earth...
>
> —**Charles Dickens**, *The Selected Letters of Charles Dickens*, edited by: Jenny Hartley.

13 Swaminarayan Temple vandalised 2019 (Kentucky) Temple in Kent, Temple in North Texas, Temple in Seattle (2015).

They were not ordinary people. Winston Churchill was the former British prime minister and Charles Dickens is considered as the greatest British writer.

Cow country

Unfortunately, Hindus are consistently shamed and ridiculed for cows and cow urine but as a global community, quite often, we fail to understand a broader perspective.

The usage of animal urine for medicinal purposes is not unique to traditional medical systems. Modern medicine also uses animal urine. The estrogen-replacement drug Premarin, prescribed to menopausal women, is made from horse urine (PETA).

So, if the global community – which likes to be known as 'progressive and modern' – is using horse-urine-based medicines, why can't Hindus use cow urine for medicinal purposes?

The Hindu traditional knowledge system of Ayurveda uses cow urine in the process of medicine preparation.[14]

Hindu knowledge systems of yoga and Ayurveda have their benefits spread across many nations and communities. The benefits of Ayurveda are also recognised and utilised by many Muslims in India.

To give you an example, the Himalaya Drug Company – which was founded by a Muslim, Mohammed Manal – uses many Ayurvedic herbs in its products and is widely popular in western nations where its Ayurvedic products are being consumed and are benefitting many Christians.[15]

14 PIB, 31 Aug, 2012, Former Union Minister Ghulam Nabi Azad in a written reply in the Lok Sabha.

15 https://www.himalayawellness.in/

Why should Hindus be mocked for research on cows?

On numerous occasions, the international media has ridiculed India for investing in research based on cows or cow products.

But when American researchers use cows to explore techniques to fight a deadly virus like HIV, nobody mocks America or its researchers (Rapid elicitation of broadly neutralising antibodies to HIV by immunisation in cows, Devin Sok and others). And nobody should. Because as a responsible global community, shouldn't we be grateful for the scientific efforts which are dedicated to treating or fighting various sicknesses and ailments? Can't we understand that diseases do not have any religion?

Animal worshipers / animals are Gods?

Hindus are also mocked because many feel that they worship cows. If worshiping cows sound irrational and unscientific to you, then so should the Christian behaviour of believing in angels.

A total of 88 per cent of Christians in America believe in angels. It should be pointed out that angels are not scientifically proven, and America is considered a modern and progressive nation which has reached the Moon and Mars (Associated Press-GfK poll). But neither Hindus nor the Indian mainstream media have systematically ridiculed anyone for their belief in angels – in contrast to the way the global community has almost shamed Hindus for their belief of a god element in cows.

Do you know that on some occasions, believing in angels has led to murders and violence, but such incidents don't quite become a global story? And they shouldn't.[16]

16 https://www.dailystar.co.uk/news/latest-news/amelia-brooke-harris-death-carly-16826550The Daily Star, UK.

Sensationalism or provocation of religious sentiments by the media and the general public must be discouraged, regardless of the religion.

As a concerned global citizen, one should realise that many behaviours and practices exist in all religions which cannot be backed by science. But why is the global community expecting Hindus to prove each and every action of theirs through science?

Furthermore, let us not forget that both religion and science can be dangerous or beneficial, it all depends on the intentions of the person who is using them.

If there is religious misconduct, there is also scientific misconduct. It should also be mentioned that cows also have a special significance for many Hindus because of the animal's association with Bhagwaan Shri Krishna (also known as Gopala), which is similar to Christians' respect for the cross because of its association with Jesus.

Official state religion

How many of us know that, despite being more than a billion in number, Hindus do not even have one country where Hinduism is an official state religion? By comparison, 13 countries including nine European nations designate Christianity or a particular Christian denomination as their state religion, and 27 countries have Islam as their state religion. Buddhism is the official religion in two countries, and in Israel, the official state religion is Judaism.

More than 80 countries favour specific religions, officially or unofficially, and India is not in that list. (Source: Pew Research Center, USA, 2017).

Despite this reality, many among these 80 countries love to preach religious freedom, tolerance and secularism within various global forums. In many countries, if you are a Hindu, you can never become the prime minster or president, as in 30 countries, heads of state must belong to some other religion, as the Pew Research Center pointed out in 2014.

What is the Swastika?

Have you seen the Swastika symbol in Hindu homes? No, it has nothing to do with Hitler and Germany. It is a sacred sign which originally belonged to India's Dharmic traditions and is many thousands of years old. So, please, let us keep our European violent history in Europe, and let us not connect it to Hindus unnecessarily.

Yoga and Hindu philosophy

For once, let us thank the Hindu community wholeheartedly for their greatest gift to mankind: Yoga. Regardless of your religion or country, please allow yourselves to benefit from this Hindu spiritual discipline. Since Hindus have no doctrine to systematically convert the non-believers, your identity and your native traditions are safe. But remember, yoga's dharmic roots cannot be denied. Essentially, yoga means experiencing union; the Dharmic thoughts of karma and reincarnation, and the idea of experiencing union are all co-related. There are various physical postures like Natrajasana or Hanumasana which clearly indicate the sacred Hindu figures.

India's dharmic traditions are also unique because they have been able to withstand the test of science and modernity. No, I am not talking about the 'father of surgery' Maharishi Sushruta, whose statue is placed in the Royal Australia College of Surgeons in Melbourne (Royal Australia College of Surgeons, Melbourne).

Neither am I talking about the renowned 18th-century English surgeon Joseph Constantine Carpue (4 May 1764 – 30 January 1846) who performed the first rhino plastic surgery in England after learning the technique from India.[17]

I am more interested in talking about things which are more relevant to our present lives, for example depression and anxiety. Hindus have an answer to those problems with yoga and meditation. You talk about global warming, pollution and greed-driven consumerism, Hindus have an answer to that with Aparigraha. Then there is the so-called modern idea of preventive health care to tackle the rising healthcare costs. The idea already pre-exists in the Hindu's Ayurveda. Let's be grateful to Hindus and give them credit where it is due.

Hindus believe in questioning and self-exploration. That is why, among Hindus, one can notice a lot of self-criticism and self-admiration. A great deal of freedom exists. There are no compulsory temple visits, no compulsory deity to worship and no compulsory book. Pray to one, all-pervasive Divine Reality or pray to its multiple manifestations; chose any of the scriptures or chose none; be an atheist or be a spiritual being. There is absolutely no compulsion for Hindus. Well, if you don't like any of the pre-existing traditions, and if your intentions are good, then create your own unique traditions. Nobody is going to stop you.

Caste system

By branding India's Jati, Kul, Varna, and Gotra as caste – a word which actually has Portuguese origins – is a reckless over-simplification.

17 Account of Two Successful Operations for Restoring a Lost Nose from the Integument of the Forehead, Joseph Constantine Carpue.

As far as birth-based discrimination is concerned, India has consistently worked on it in a very complex political atmosphere and it still remains a work in progress. India has made significant improvements in that regard. The members from the so called 'backward or low caste' communities have already held top ranks such as: chief minister, president and prime minster. So I urge the global community to act responsibly by properly studying the subject of caste from genuine sources before making a statement on the so-called 'caste system'.

Pluralism and tolerance

Don't you think that if we truly believe in pluralism and tolerance, we should also accept Hindus the way they are, without being intolerant of their Gods by calling them 'false Gods', and by not shaming Hindus for their unique ways of worship.

Lisa Jane Miller is a professor who is best known as a research scholar on spirituality in psychology.

She writes:

> The Rig Veda, the most ancient Hindu scripture, says this: 'Truth is One, but the sages speak of it by many names.' A Hindu believes there are many paths to God. Jesus is one way, the Qur'an is another, yoga practice is a third. None is better than any other; all are equal. The most traditional, conservative Christians have not been taught to think like this. They learn in Sunday school that their religion is true, and others are false. Jesus said, 'I am the way, the truth, and the life. No one comes to the father except through me'.

What Professor Miller has written can actually be confirmed by a random visit to various worship places in India. One can find the followers of India's Dharmic traditions praying in Hindu or Jain temples, Buddhist temples, Gurudwaras, Muslim shrines, and even Churches. It is the spiritual awareness of a typical Hindu which enables him or her to find divinity everywhere. On the other hand, the followers of non-dharmic systems cannot be easily spotted in Dharmic places of worship.

Give it a thought: Is being 'tolerant' really that respectful? For instance, can you tell your guests who visit your home that you are tolerating them? Obviously not! That is why a step far higher than that is to be 'accommodating and accepting'.

The fact that Hindus are the most 'accommodating and accepting' is also supported by an American research which revealed that 73 per cent of Asian-American Hindus celebrate Christmas and 30 per cent of them sometimes attend services of other religions. The research revealed: 'Hindus tend to be inclusive in their understanding of faith.' An overwhelming 91 per cent of Asian-American Hindus believe that many religions can lead to eternal life. On the other hand, 72 per cent of Asian-American evangelicals say that their religion is the one, true faith (Pew Research Center, 2012).

Now this explains clearly why Indian shopping malls are almost completely covered with Christmas decorations even though Christians number just around two per cent of the country's population (Census 2011). On the other hand, with nearly 2 per cent of Hindus in Australia and around two per cent of Hindus in New Zealand, how many shopping malls in those countries are covered with grand Deepawali decorations? (New Zealand, 2013 Census, Australia, 2016 Census.)

I have personally seen many Hindu homes in which a photo of Jesus Christ sits right next to Krishna and other Hindu deities while they pray to all of them; still we Europeans try to preach tolerance to Indians.

For those who believe in the idea of global conquest by their religious monoculture, how can they even claim to believe in the idea of the co-existence of multiple cultures? For those who want exclusivity and expansion, how can they claim to support multiple paths and views?

Promoting religious monoculture kills diversity. If diversity dies, the idea of pluralism dies to.

The biggest paradox of the 21st century is that monotheistic ideologies are trying to preach to us the importance of pluralism.

It doesn't mean that Hinduism is perfect, and Hindus can't learn from others. Hinduism could learn from Christianity how to effectively and efficiently keep the members of their community well informed and well connected.

From Islam, Hinduism could learn the willingness to protect its own interests if and when required.

But as a global community, whether we admit it or not, in one way or the other, many among us are already beneficiaries of some type of Hindu heritage.

Whenever we promote the ancient pranayama technique as 'cardiac coherence breathing' or teach meditation to our school children as 'mindfulness classes', we are creating a new tradition for ourselves, similar to that which already exists in ancient Hindu traditions.[18]

India's Dharmic traditions encourage people to focus on conquering their own mind and to reject the idea of conquering the world.

Can the world afford to see Hindu culture, wisdom and intellectual traditions disappear?

---

18 Proper Breathing Brings Better Health, Scientific American, By Christophe André, Source: Schools in England Introduce a New Subject: Mindfulness, By Iliana Magra, NYTimes.

FOUR

A TOURIST'S PARADISE 2018-19

India has a beautiful national tourism policy that wants 'to ensure that the tourists to India get physically invigorated, mentally rejuvenated, culturally enriched, spiritually elevated and feel India from within'.

IN MOST countries, travel and tourism is a major engine of economic growth and India is no exception.

It affects all segments of the society by creating large-scale employment and by positively affecting various sectors of the economy. In 2015, International tourist arrivals in India were more than 13 million. In 2016, there were more than 14 million out of which Foreign Tourist arrivals (FTAs) were 8.8 million and NRI arrivals were more than 5 million, says the Bureau of Immigration, Govt of India.

In 2017, the number of foreign tourist arrivals crossed the 10 million mark.

In 2016, Tamil Nadu had the greatest number of foreign tourist visits, and it was closely followed by Maharashtra. Tamil Nadu is also ahead of every other state in India when it comes to domestic tourists' visits.

Globally, there were more than 1.2 billion international tourist arrivals in 2016. Out of that, India's share was just 1.18 per cent. In terms of international tourist arrivals, India is placed at 25th position globally (2016).

In terms of international tourism receipts, it is placed at 13th position (2016).[1]

According to a report by WTTC (World Travel and Tourism Council), in 2016, travel and tourism directly and indirectly generated $208 billion and supported over 40 million jobs.

India's travel and tourism sector is dominated by domestic travelers who accounted for 88 per cent of the sector's contribution to GDP in 2016. In 2016, the total number of domestic tourists in India was over 1.6 billion.[2]

India's rank has been constantly improving in the Travel & Tourism Competitiveness Index (TTCI). In 2017, India was placed at 40th position as compared to 52nd in 2015 and 65th in 2013.

By 2027, the sector's (travel and tourism) total contribution to GDP is expected to grow to USD 424 billion and by 2030, India is expected to be ranked among the top five business travel market.[3] India is also witnessing a digital revolution.

---

1 India Tourism Statistics At a Glance, 2017, Govt of India.
2 Source: State/Union Territory Tourism Departments.
3 World Travel and Tourism Council.

It has expanded its E-visa scheme, it has introduced an e-FRRO (Foreign Registration Office) facility for foreign nationals, and it has been aggressively improving its physical and digital infrastructure.

In terms of tourism products, India is blessed with an extremely diverse portfolio which includes wellness, adventure, sports, eco-tourism, cruise tourism, spiritual tourism and film tourism.

India is a 365-day destination. It has 29 States, nine union territories, 4000 cities, 600,000 villages, 26 biotic provinces, 10 bio-geographical zones and more than 30 World Heritage sites (UNESCO).

The North East Region of India has eight States: Arunachal Pradesh, Assam, Manipur, Meghalaya, Mizoram, Nagaland, Tripura and Sikkim. They are said to be India's hidden gems. Their unique tribal cultures, striking flora and fauna, music, folk dancing and indigenous sports can easily tempt any traveller.

With its 7,000 km coastline, as well as its mountains, deserts, rainforests, islands, volcanoes, salt flats, wildlife, and tribal habitation, India is incredibly diversified.

International hotel brands have been rapidly expanding their presence in India. The country has thousands of heritage hotels which makes it a paradise for destination weddings.

By 2025, India's international arrivals will reach 15.3 million and it is expected that India will have the largest civil aviation market by 2030.[4]

Well, it all sounds pretty favourable but there is something that is equally important. And that is safety and security.

Here is a list of top ten source countries where India gets its foreign tourists from.

---

4 Source: The Aviation Industry Leaders Report 2018: KPMG.

Top 10 Source Countries for Foreign Tourist Arrivals (FTAs) in India in 2016			
S. No	**Source Country**	**FTAs**	**Percentage (%) Share**
1	Bangladesh	1380409	15.68
2	United States	1296939	14.73
3	United Kingdom	941883	10.70
4	Canada	317239	3.60
5	Malaysia	301961	3.43
6	Sri Lanka	297418	3.38
7	Australia	293625	3.33
8	Germany	265928	3.02
9	China	251313	2.85
10	France	238707	2.71
	Total top 10 Countries	5585422	63.44
	Others	3218989	36.56
	G.Total	**8804411**	**100.00**

Source: Bureau of Immigration, Govt. of India

It is apparant that India gets a lot of visitors from the US and the UK. Now, let's check how safe India is for the citizens of these two countries.

Here is a list of the foreign countries in which the most American civilians were killed between October 2009 and June 2016 (in per capita terms). India is nowhere on the list.

Top 25 Countries by Americans Killed Per Capita

Rank	Country	American Travelers	Americans Killed	Per Capita
1	Pakistan	226,200	8	3.54
2	Thailand	343,500	11	3.2
3	Philippines	3,240,000	74	2.28
4	Haiti	3,316,700	65	1.96
5	Honduras	2,766,800	46	1.66
6	Nigeria	780,900	10	1.28
7	Belize	1,563,400	16	1.02
8	Guyana	722,200	7	0.97
9	Egypt	579,800	5	0.86
10	Mexico	71,608,500	598	0.84
11	Guatemala	3,799,600	26	0.68
12	El Salvador	5,324,400	34	0.64
13	Greece	691,800	3	0.43
14	Jordan	775,600	3	0.39
15	Jamaica	10,606,600	39	0.37
16	Ukraine	276,800	1	0.36
17	Ecuador	3,457,500	12	0.35
18	Nicaragua	2,060,000	7	0.34
19	Costa Rica	8,137,400	27	0.33
20	Grenada	328,900	1	0.3
21	Colombia	8,677,700	25	0.29
22	Uruguay	355,200	1	0.28
23 (tie)	Barbados	1,468,600	4	0.27
23 (tie)	Saudi Arabia	749,100	2	0.27
24	Dominican Republic	18,169,700	45	0.25

Source/data.world

The figures were obtained through a Freedom of Information request to the Foreign Office by MailOnline (per capita figures could not be found).

And here is a list of ten countries in which the highest number of British people were killed between 2012 and August 2015. Again, India is nowhere on the list.

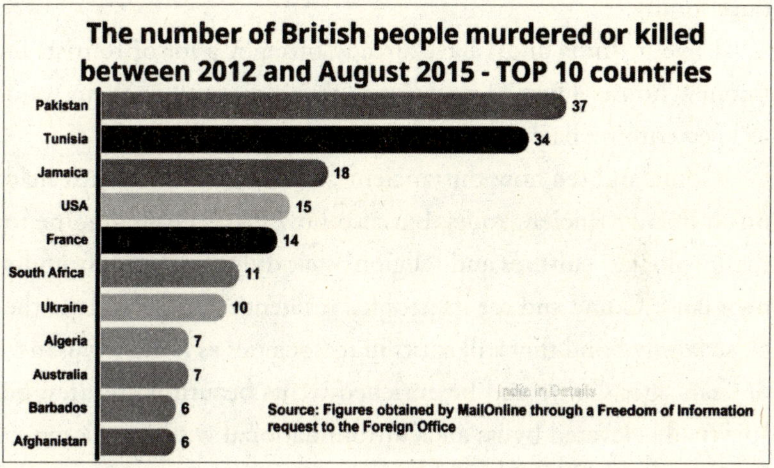

Tourism is a significant source of foreign exchange earnings and up to 1/10th of global GDP and jobs are tourism-related (WEF).

Tourism has a great capacity to bring human prosperity. It creates opportunities for a positive cultural exchange, and it strengthens people to people relations.

It helps in poverty eradication and it brings socioeconomic benefits for those at the bottom of the pyramid.

Directly or indirectly, travel and tourism brings empowerment to all sections of society. It creates large-scale employment by increasing the demand for unskilled, semi-skilled and skilled workers.

Every tourist who comes to India presents multiple possibilities which are visible and invisible. Many people come as tourists but end up becoming partners in trade and business. Often, those who have a good time come back and revisit. And if they are not able to revisit, they might end up sending others.

I love India for its radiant historical and cultural heritage, for its diversity in ecology and cuisine, and most significantly for its spiritually harmonious roots that encourage self-exploration and questioning.

I live in India and I have already brought a lot of tourists to my new home. There is no surprise that almost all of them want to keep coming back.

Come and see how this ancient civilisation has not just held on to its own ancient roots, but also how it has given a home to the ideologies, cultures and religions that didn't originate from its own land. Come and see its people's resilience. Come and see the close family bond that still exists in its societies as it did thousands of years ago. Come and be enriched by its beautiful cultures; be spiritually elevated by its ancient foundational wisdom. Come to India to 'feel India from within'.

India's North Eastern region

Arunachal Pradesh, Assam, Manipur, Meghalaya, Mizoram, Nagaland, Tripura and Sikkim are India's eight north eastern States which in true sense are the country's hidden gems.

Diversity in ecology, culture and ethnicity makes this area very unique. It is quite reasonable to say that the north eastern region of India is one of the most underestimated tourist destinations in the entire world.

The land of red rivers and blue hills, the land of the rising sun, the land of peace and tranquility, the abode of clouds...yes, these phrases do justice to the beauty and uniqueness of India's north eastern States, which are considered to be among the most bio-diverse regions in the world. Historically, forests, agriculture and other natural resources played a significant role in the cultural landscape of the region which gave birth to a very rich tribal heritage. Indigenous religious traditions, cultures and crafts flourished, because the region managed to remain untouched by western religious and commercial monocultures for a very long time.

The north eastern region of India is not an ordinary place by any means.

India is the second-largest producer of silk in the world, and its north-eastern States are among the biggest contributors (Central Silk Board, Ministry of Textiles, Govt of India).

Tripura is the second-largest natural rubber producer in the country (Ministry of Agriculture)

Assam has the largest tea-growing area in the world, with about one-seventh of the global tea production. Fifty per cent of the country's overall tea production takes place in Assam (Government of Assam).

In terms of bamboo genetic resources, India is the second-richest country in the world after China (FAO report, World Forest Resources). Over 50 per cent of bamboo species occur in eastern India (Forest Survey of India).

The whole region is endowed with deposits of various minerals, and many of them are not yet fully explored.

The first oil well in Asia was drilled in Assam, and the State is also the third-largest producer of petroleum and natural gas in India (Government of Assam).With its 600 million tonnes of oil and gas reserves, Nagaland alone could boost India's onshore oil and gas production by 75 per cent (Nagaland State Mineral Development Corporation Limited). Arunachal Pradesh alone has more than one third of the country's total identified hydropower potential above 25 MW (50,328 MW of the country's total 148,701 MW identified hydropower potential) according to the Central Electricity Authority. When it comes to physical infrastructure, a lot of work is in progress.

In Manipur, the world's tallest railway bridge and India's longest tunnel are under construction (Govt of Manipur / Indian Railways).

A trilateral agreement with Thailand and Myanmar is in place to construct a trans-Asian highway, which will connect India (via Manipur) to the two countries, and will make the region a real gateway to east and south-east Asia.

The region already has the longest rail-cum-road bridge in the country (Bogibeel, as on Dec 2018). It is considered to be one of the 'biodiversity hotspots' of the world, and it supports about 50 per cent of India's biodiversity.

It supports one of the highest bird diversities in the East, with about 850 of the 1,200 bird species known on the Indian subcontinent.[5]

Of the nine important vegetation types of India, six are found in the north eastern region (Hegde 2000).

The region is the center of origin of citrus fruits, it is rich in wild relatives of crop plants, and it has been identified as a center of rice germplasm (National Bureau of Plant Genetic Resources, Indian Council of Agricultural Research). Sixteen of India's 104 national parks are located in its eight north-eastern states (National Wildlife Database Cell, Wildlife Institute of India). The entire Eastern Himalayas region was identified in the WWF's Global 200 ecoregion list, and Conservational International included the entire eight states of the North East in its Eastern Himalaya

5 India-Development and Growth in Northeast India: The Natural Resources, Water, and Environment Nexus, A World Bank Report.

Hotspot. In physiographical terms, the region can be categorised into the Northeast Hills (Lushai Hills and Patkai-Naga Hills), the Eastern Himalayas, and the Brahmaputra and Barak Valley plains.

Sikkim has the world's third-highest peak: the Kanchenjunga. Meghalaya has some of the deepest and longest caves in South Asia.

Tropical rain forests, alpine meadows, cold deserts...the region is truly blessed. With as many as 8,000 species, India is the world's second-largest exporter of medicinal plants.

Forty thousand herbal formulations derived from these medicinal plants form the backbone of India's rich, traditional medicine-based health care system. Hundreds of medicinal plants are native to the north eastern region of India.

The traditional tribal homes are relevant today. They demonstrate original sustainable living, and sophisticated engineering skills. In Nagland, during discussions with the local people it was noted that the majority of the traditional houses 'survived' during major earthquakes in the past. In India the number of individual groups which are registered as scheduled tribes is around 700 (Census of India 2011 / Draft National Tribal Policy, 2006).

States like Odisha, Karnataka, Maharashtra top the list. Nearly 140 tribal communities (notified STs) live in the eight north-eastern states of India (Tribal-Committee-Report-May-June-2014).

The region is a melting pot with multiple ethnicities, cultures and religions. The total population of north-east India is 46 million, and 68 per cent of that population resides in Assam(2011 census).

There are about 220 languages spoken in these states, belonging to multiple language families (1971 census).

Sikkim

Sikkim, the world's first 100 per cent organic state has become the role model for the entire world in organic farming, say no less an entity like the FAO.

Unique environmental conditions for the development of floriculture makes it the 'Kingdom of Flowers', says the Indian Horticulture Database 2014-National Horticulture Board.

India is the largest producer of large cardamom in the world. A vast majority (around 80) of that is produced in Sikkim (Ministry of Agriculture, GoI).

The state is known for its Buddhist monasteries, Himalayan flora and fauna and for its unique Temi tea.

Eighty-four glaciers, 315 glacial lakes, 10 mountain peaks, five hot springs, eight mountain passes, 200 monasteries. This place is a paradise for tourists (Govt of Sikkim).

Meghalaya

Mawsynram (Meghalaya) is the wettest place in the world. Mawlynnong was declared the cleanest village in Asia.

The crystal-clear water of the Umngot river, living root bridges, one of the world's oldest golf courses, some of the deepest and longest caves in South Asia, a solid school and college infrastructure...there is no other place like Meghalaya in the entire world.

One of the fascinating sides of Meghalaya is the tribal community, Garo. They are one of the few remaining matrilineal societies in the world. Overall, matrilineal system is not too uncommon in the state.

Their traditional tribal architecture is an excellent example of vernacular architecture, which should serve as an inspiration for everyone who is involved in sustainable construction and architecture.

Tripura

This state has cultural ties with Bengal and other tribal regions of Assam, Manipur and Mizoram. The Tripuris are the largest tribal community. This beautiful hilly state is known for its rock cut carvings, ancient temples and the famous Ujjayanta Palace, which was built by Maharaja Radha Kishore Manikya (during 1899-1901).

Arunachal Pradesh

Arunachal Pradesh gets a mention in 'Kalika and Mahabharata', which are Dharmic literature from ancient India. One of the oldest and the largest Buddhist monasteries (Tawang) is situated in Arunachal Pradesh (Govt of Arunachal Pradesh).

The state is also the birth place of the sixth Dalai Lama.

Life-transforming and self-awakening moments in such a tranquil setting come naturally.

Assam

Kaziranga National Park and the Manas Wildlife Sanctuary are UNESCO World Heritage sites. There was a time when Assam's famous one-horned rhino was close to extinction. The conservation of the one-horned Indian rhino in the last few decades is a phenomenal success story, says the Rhino Vision 2020 Population Modeling Workshop, November 2014 report.

Sattriya dance from Assam is one of the most important Indian classical dances. Shri Ghanakanta Bora Muktiyar is one of the most eminent gurus of Sattriya dance.

His home is Guwahati – the most populous city of the entire north eastern region, and the land of Goddess Kamakhya, whose temple is one of the oldest Shakti Peeths of India.

Each folk dance from Assam has a deep meaning and a fascinating story of its evolution.

Assam's traditional tribal homes are some of the finest examples of India's rich heritage: a combination of intelligent engineering and sustainable living. Totally relevant in the 21st century, there is a lot to learn from and admire in these communities, which are culturally very advanced.

Manipur

A 90-minute drive from the largest freshwater lake in north-east India brings you to Imphal, the capital city of Manipur.

The most important landmark – and a symbol of Manipur's ancient glory – is located close to the banks of the Imphal river: Kangla Palace.

For centuries, this land was an epicenter of political, religious and cultural activities. Unfortunately, it also became a target for invaders. Manipuri rulers faced invasions and hostility from Burma and the British.

The British occupied Kangla Fort in 1891, and they destroyed two massive iconic 'Kangla Sha'. Today, in independent India, they stand tall, fully restored and rebuilt, reflecting the golden heritage of Manipur.

Vaishnavism is one of the most important Vedic traditions, and Manipur is one of the most important historical centers.

Ras-Lila, a classical Indian dance form, has its roots in Manipur. In the entire north-eastern region of India, Manipur has the highest number of handicraft units and skilled handicraft artisans (Govt of India). Some of these exquisite Manipuri handlooms and other household items can be purchased in a unique all-women market run by more than 3,000 women.

Ima means mother, and this market is called 'Ima Keithel (Mothers' Market)'.

The beautiful traditional costume that is commonly seen on Manipuri women is called Phanek. Whether college girls or professionals, 'it is loved by everyone, and it is a significant component of Manipuri dress and culture'.

Friendly Manipuri people open their homes and hearts for their guests. Their simplicity and hospitality are absolutely heart-warming.

It is no surprise that Manipur is known as 'the Jewel of India'.

Mizoram

Many foreign tourists may not even know where Mizoram is, and how friendly and hard-working the Mizo people are. The state has the highest concentration of protected tribal people (scheduled tribe) in India, and today, almost all of them are Christians (2011 census, GoI).

You will find either a musician or a footballer in virtually every other home. Many emerging and well-known footballers in India are from this state. In the future, if India improves its football infrastructure, its stature will grow in the world of football, and Mizoram will very likely play a key role in this.

Nagaland

Nagaland – a predominantly tribal state, which is situated on India's eastern border, has gained popularity in recent years. During World War II, the Japanese invaded India, which at that time was a colony of Britain. Kohima in Nagaland was an important battlefield in 1944.

Since then, Nagaland has come a long way.

The cultural wealth of Nagaland is very visible during the annual Hornbill Festival, which is attended by many tourists from all over the world.

To my mind, there is no other place in the world that can match India's north eastern states. They represent our planet's hidden treasure.

Yes, it may be true that western commercial and religious monocultures have diluted many indigenous traditions, as well as the diversity in this region, however, the land is still culturally rich and diverse. After interacting with hundreds of locals and spending a lot of time in the region, I barely scratched the surface.

There is a lot that we can learn from these people. Their resilience, simplicity and hospitality can touch anyone in so many more ways than I can articulate. These eight north-eastern states are India's hidden gems.

India as an expat destination

There is no denying that India is emerging as a lucrative expat destination. It is the 12th best country to live in as an expat. It is far ahead of countries like the USA (23rd), the UK (22nd), Japan (30th) and China (27th), according to HSBC's Expat Explorer Survey 2018.

India-based expats earn an average of USD 176,408, which means that they are the second-highest paid in the world, says the suvey. In 2017, India shot up by 12 spots to reach 14th position in the Expat Explorer League table which reflects India's dramatic emergence as a top expat destination. The country not only provides handsome financial opportunities to expats, but it also has a great impact on their family life. In 2017, the country ranked second in bringing expat couples closer together, as 54 per cent of expats felt closer to their partner after their arrival in India.

Moving away from your country can be difficult, especially for younger kids who often find it challenging to make new friends. In that respect, India provides a very favourable atmosphere. When it comes to finding friends for children of expats, India ranks third globally, the survey notes.

India-based expats have high levels of confidence in the country's economy, and for many of them India provides a very promising atmosphere in which to start a new business. The HSBC's Expat Explorer Survey 2017 also revealed that more than half of expats who were living in India in 2017 felt that the country is a good place to start a business.

A lower cost of living means more disposable income. Most expats feel that their life in India can help build their personal wealth. Seventy seven per cent of expats in India own property somewhere in the world, in comparison to the global average of 62 per cent.

India provides a great platform in terms of professional development; in 2017, the country ranked seventh in terms of career progression.

Expats in India hail from all over the world, and thanks to India's favourable atmosphere, almost half of them have children with them, which is one of the highest proportions in the world. All this data come from the HSBC's Expat Explorer Survey 2018 too.

Progress in your professional career, improvement in your personal relationship, fast wealth generation: India offers multiple opportunities and a unique experience that cannot be matched anywhere else.

India's rich culture and its spiritual foundational wisdom are its big assets; the country's ancient tradition of welcoming guests is deeply ingrained in its society.

Whether you are unsettled by your country's political or economic instability, or whether you are looking to speed up your journey to prosperity, India is more than ready to accommodate you, reward you and make you feel at home.

India – a responsible power

2008 – China is struck by a major earthquake. India offers USD 5 million to China for its relief activities for the victims of the earthquake(MEA).

2005 – Pakistan is struck by an earthquake. India offers USD 25 million to the Pakistani government as a cash assistance along with USD 15 million in 'in-kind'contributions from both private and governmental sources.[6]

2010 – Pakistan is suffering from massive floods. This time, India offers USD 25 million to Pakistan to help the victims of flood. Again, India comes to the rescue of its so called 'arch rival' (MEA).

2005 – An Indian Air Force aircraft arrives at the Little Rock Air Force Base in Arkansas in the USA. It is carrying 25 tons of relief supplies for victims of Hurricane Katrina.

On multiple occasions, Sri Lanka has received humanitarian assistance from India worth more than USD 120 million (CSR Murthy 2011).

In March, 2017, it was revealed (India's Minister of State of its Ministry of External Affairs, Parliament Q & A) that India had been a net donor of foreign aid in the last three years; it had provided more aid to foreign countries, than it had received. Not only that, in 2004, when India was itself affected by a tsunami, it

6 Kelman 2006: 223, Chandran et al 2009: 69-70, C.S.R. Murthy 2011.

still went on to send help to other nations like Thailand, Indonesia and Sri Lanka. It deployed 14 Navy vessels, nearly 1,000 military personnel, and several dozen helicopters and airplanes to Sri Lanka (MEA, Dr Constantino Xavier).

It does not matter what part of the world it is. Africa, America or anywhere else, if there is a crisis, India is often seen as the first country responding to it. During the 2010 Yemen crisis, more than 25 countries asked for help from India to rescue their citizens and help them to evacuate. Germany, USA, Sweden, France...just to name a few (MEA).

As recently as 2015, India extricated nearly 2,000 nationals who belonged to 48 different countries (MEA), including many from the United States, the European Union and its neighboring countries. In most cases, it is India's Navy, its Air Force, its national airline (Air India) and its ministry of external affairs which handle such operations.

It does not matter whether it is a high-risk conflict zone or a post-natural disaster area, India is always there for the nations suffering from a crisis.

Apart from providing 'cash assistance', 'food assistance' and 'humanitarian assistance' it also partners many nations in post-calamity recovery and in various development projects. India has 279 LOCs (lines of credit) which are worth USD 28 billion in 63 nations in Africa, Asia, Latin America, the Caribbean, and Oceania. 'Of this, 254 projects aggregating nearly USD 4.70 billion have been completed, while 194 projects worth nearly USD 19 billion are under implementation. These include 94 connectivity projects in five countries in India's immediate neighbourhood being taken up with LOC worth nearly $6.6 billion (V Muraleedharan, June 2019, Parliament of India).'

Whether it is search and rescue missions or more uncommon situations like combating piracy in the Gulf of Aden where India sent almost 30 warships, escorting more than 1,500 ships, and blocking nearly 30 piracy attempts (MEA), its army is globally admired for its humanitarian nature and for its potency.

How many of us know that the Reserve Bank of India provided financial assistance to the governments of Maldives, Bhutan, and Sri Lanka when they faced foreign currency liquidity shortage?(RBI)

How many of us know that India is one of the largest contributors to the United Nations peacekeeping missions?(UN)

Whether it is Sri Lanka, Afghanistan or Nepal, in post conflict scenarios, India is often seen extending its long-term support to facilitate reconstruction and stabilisation.

In South Asia, if any crisis emerges and if people fear for their lives, they look to India first – a nation which, since time immemorial, has provided a sanctuary to those affected by any type of persecution.

The UN has even praised India's efforts by citing its refugee policy as a model for other countries (Antonio Guterres, UN).

Whenever a country asks India to mediate and help in reaching peaceful settlements, India plays a constructive role. Its experts provide technical assistance to other countries in designing new constitutions and also in helping them to hold elections smoothly (Constantino Xavier, MEA).

Globally, India is involved in assisting other countries in infrastructure development. But what makes India even more special is its keenness to help other countries to become self-dependent in the long run. A good example of that is India's Pan-African e-network which was built at a cost of USD 125 million and encompasses more than 48 African nations, bridging the digital divide and providing top quality education and training. It was the brainchild of former Indian president A P J Abdul Kalam (MEA).

India also provides scholarships to many foreign nationals, and in 2011 during the India-Africa Forum Summit, it pledged USD 5 billion in aid to Africa in the form of concessional loans.

And let us not forget that globally, most countries are beneficiaries of India's cheap medicinal drugs which have saved millions of lives.

India's style of foreign aid is quite different from the western countries, which generally provide conditional aid. India respects the sovereignty of other countries and, unlike many other nations, Indian aid programmes are not designed to interfere with the beneficiary's domestic policies or its demographics.

India's cultural and spiritual values are all about humanitarianism. India believes in the selfless nature of giving. India's foundational wisdom of universal brotherhood is reflected in its actions.

FIVE

INDIA: THE PHARMACY OF THE WORLD

Yusuf Khwaja Hamied, the chairman of Cipla (an Indian multinational pharmaceutical and biotechnology company), is a well-known Indian scientist and a billionaire businessman. Against all odds, he succeeded in providing lifesaving drugs to those who needed them the most.

In 2001, Cipla came up with the world's first ever recommended three-in-one fixed-dose combination (stavudine + lamivudine + nevirapine) to fight AIDS. It was made available at less than $1 per day – far lower than the other available treatment at the time which cost over $12,000 per patient per year. This brave act "lifted the death sentence from millions across the developing world' (Cipla).

Nicknamed 'India's Robin Hood of drugs', the company has saved millions of lives in Africa and in other parts of the world by providing world class medicine at affordable prices. 'I don't want to make money off these diseases which cause the whole fabric of society to crumble' says Hamied.

GLOBALLY, PROVIDING effective healthcare continues to be an ongoing challenge. In a survey that was conducted in 2015, 26 per cent of Americans said that someone in their household is struggling to pay medical debt (Kaiser/New York Times Survey).

In 2017, 10.9 million people in the USA were pushed below the poverty line because of out-of-pocket medical costs, says the US Census Bureau, Current Population Survey, 2018 Annual Social and Economic Supplement.

Nearly 80 per cent of US workers live paycheck to paycheck in order to make ends meet (Career Builder, 2017). A report revealed that 46 per cent of Americans could not even cover a $400 emergency expense. They would have to cover it by selling something or by borrowing money, says the Report on the Economic Well-Being of US Households in 2015, Federal Reserve Board, DCCA.Even those Americans who have health insurance often find it difficult to pay the amount (deductible) that is required before the insurance plan starts to pay. It was found that half of all insurance policy holders in the USA faced a deductible of at least $1,000, says the KFF, 2016 Employer Health Benefits Survey.

An amount of $1000 is already too much for many Americans to have in their bank savings. In 2016, a survey by GoBankingRates revealed that 34 per cent of Americans have no money in the bank and 69 per cent of Americans do not even have $1,000 in savings.

This means that they will be unable to pay a $1000 health insurance deductible in the event of an emergency.There is no denying that medical bills are considered to be one of the main reasons of bankruptcies in the US. In England, half a million patients had to wait for more than 18 weeks to start planned treatment (NHS England 'referral to treatment', RTT statistics for April 2018).

In Canada, a study revealed that an estimated 731,000 Canadians had to borrow money to buy prescription drugs. They were also forced to give up their basic necessities.[1] The Commonwealth Fund's 2016 International Health Policy Survey found out that one out of two Canadians had to wait for four or more weeks to see a specialist and one out of three Canadians has to wait for more than four hours in the emergency rooms.

According to the Fraser institute, the total number of procedures for which people in Canada were waiting in 2016 was almost a million (973,505). (CT scan – 3.7 weeks, ultrasound – 4.0 weeks, MRI scan- 11.1 weeks, year- 2016.)

Not just that, just a simple admission in hospital can make Canadians wait for many days; for home care services, the wait time can be in months and for a patient who needs a long-term care bed, wait time can be in years.

According to Merritt Hawkins' 2017 Survey, wait times to see a physician in the US have increased. In Boston it is more than 52 days for an average new patient and the overall average wait is 24 days. In the UK, the National Health Service (NHS), which has a workforce of 1.5 million, is struggling too, as in 2016, on an average, almost 200,000 (193,406) people a month did not get surgery, even after waiting for more than four and a half months, according to none other than the Royal College of Surgeons. India is the top supplier of doctors to both the UK and the USA (International Migration Outlook 2015, OECD).

---

1 Source: Patterns of borrowing to finance out-of-pocket prescription drug costs in Canada: a descriptive analysis Ashra Kolhatkar MPH, Lucy Cheng MSc, Steven G Morgan PhD, Laurie J Goldsmith PhD, Irfan A Dhalla MD MSc, Anne M Holbrook MD PharmD, Michael R Law PhD.

Many doctors and nurses of Indian origin are not only treating patients abroad, but through its solid medical tourism industry and its pharma industry, India has also been helping many citizens of the developed, developing and poor parts of the world in their healing journey.

With more than 500,000 foreign patients seeking treatment annually, India is an important medical tourism destination (FICCI, Medical Value Travel In India).

The quality of treatment in India is world-class and the costs are very low (medicaltourism.com). In addition, India's ancient healing systems, which includes the likes of Ayruveda and Sidhha, make the country even more unique.

In many western countries, dental work, cosmetic surgeries, and many life-saving drugs, are not covered by insurance and not everyone has a medical insurance.

In terms of producing medicines, India is far ahead of China, which mostly produces API (active pharmaceutical ingredients). API are actually the raw ingredients of medicines. India also purchases API from China, and in the past, India was the main source of API itself. India is also looking for ways to reduce its purchase of API from China. The country is not only capable of manufacturing API itself, but it also does not see China as a very reliable partner, as its relations with this country is both sweet and sour.

Twenty-five per cent of all medicines in the UK are sourced from India; 40 per cent of generic drugs taken by Americans are made in India, and India's massive pharmaceutical industry is the source of more than 50 per cent of global demand for various vaccines (Pharmexcil, GoI.)

In 2016, India was the top supplier to the United Nations with $804 million sales in pharmaceuticals and medical services.

In order to provide affordable life-saving drugs to millions of poor people, India refused to recognise pharmaceutical patents for more than three decades. In 1995, it joined World Trade Organisation (WTO) and then it changed its patent policy. However, India's patent law (2005) does not allow 'evergreening', which is a tricky way that drug companies use to secure a new patent by making minor adjustments in existing drugs. And the western drug companies do not like it.

Yes, India makes generic medicines, but generic medicines are produced in Europe too. Yes, pharmaceutical companies have lost patent cases in India, but they have also lost cases in Europe and even in the US. India has every right to have a strict patent law and it also has every right to have a special clause of 'compulsory licensing' which saves the lives of millions of people around the world, who would otherwise die without lifesaving drugs.[2]

And anyway, since 2005, India has also issued hundreds of patents to many foreign drug companies, including the patent that it granted to US pharma giant Pfizer for its pneumonia vaccine in 2017.

However, USA continues to keep India on the 'priority watch list (PWL) category" in the US Trade Representative (USTR) report, a category that also includes China.

Yes, the USA's frustration regarding China is understandable as somehow, China has adopted a strategy of 'fake it until you make it' with all its counterfeit goods industries and hackers.

But why should India be blamed for providing affordable medicines and saving millions of lives? Does it sound legitimate?

---

2 Compulsory licensing – The term Compulsory Licensing is used when 'a government allows someone else to produce the patented product or process without the consent of the patent owner'.

And anyways, the USA must remember its own history before it blames anyone. Should we forget how one of the founding fathers of the USA, Alexander Hamilton, in his 1791 'Report of Manufactures' wanted his country to reward those who brought 'improvements and secrets of extraordinary value' from elsewhere?

Or should we forget how Francis Cabot Lowell stole the designs for the power loom from Britain in 1810 and brought the industrial revolution to America? Or how about Charles Dickens, an English writer who went to America, intending to launch his new novel but found that pirate copies had already been on sale for months? (Source: Mary Bellis).

Or how about Thomas Digges, an industrial spy from America? He was jailed by the British but praised by George Washington for his special efforts.

There is a reason why the historian Doron Ben-Atar wrote in his book, *Trade Secrets*, 'The United States emerged as the world's industrial leader by illicitly appropriating mechanical and scientific innovations from Europe'.

The British are also renowned for their deeds. Robert Fortune, who was an industrial spy of the East India Company was sent to China to steal the complex technique for processing tea leaves, points out Sarah Rose in her book, *For All the Tea in China: How England Stole the World's Favorite Drink and Changed History.*

Even the first factory of the United Kingdom was built thanks to the illicit diagrams of an Italian silk mill. Thomas Lombe – the man who set up this factory was even knighted.

This trend continues today. It was estimated that in 2005, about 2,000 patents were granted globally which were related to Indian systems of medicine – India's traditional intellectual heritage , according to TKDL.

But the western media largely remains silent on such issues.

Why did it not create sensational headlines in the UK when Pangaea Laboratories Limited, a UK-based company was caught stealing a formula from Ayurveda and was trying to patent it?

Why did it not create sensational headlines in the USA when Colgate-Palmolive was caught stealing and patenting a formula from Indian traditional systems of medicine in their mouthwash? (PIB, India.)

For thousands of years Indians have been freely sharing their knowledge of Ayurveda with everyone but the western idea to convert an open source and affordable Indian Ayruvedic formula into a high-end luxurious patented organic beauty product is illegitimate, greed-driven and self-serving. Not only that, such an act doesn't resonate with the Indian traditional principle of '*Sarwe Bhavantu Sukhinaha*'.

On the contrary, Indians drug companies are converting the unaffordable lifesaving drugs into affordable, high-quality medicines, which are saving millions of lives globally, including many lives in the developed world.

Yes, the R&D cost of inventing a new drug can be high, but if the USA can spend 600 billion USD for its defense annually so that it can establish 'peace' in the world through its weapons, it can surely also do something to protect its own people who are dying without proper healthcare system and can try to bring down the prices of life-saving drugs.

India's overall role in global healthcare may sound very optimistic, but has the country done enough to provide its citizens with a robust healthcare system? No, not yet. The work is still in progress.

The vast majority of India's population depends on the country's private healthcare sector and in most cases, healthcare expenses are paid out of pocket by patients and their families.

Out-of-pocket health expenses pushed 55 million Indians into poverty in 2011-12.[3]

In 2014, a survey by NSSO (India's sample survey organisation) found that 82 per cent of the urban population and 86 per cent of the rural population was not covered under any scheme of health expenditure support. However, it is important to point out that 75 per cent of urban households and 68 per cent of rural households in India were able to cover their hospitalisation expenditure using their income and savings (the NSS 71st Round).

However, it must be pointed out that many states in India are running their own state-specific healthcare initiatives, and in 2018, the country launched an ambitious nationwide scheme (Ayushman Bharat) which is said to be the world's biggest government health programme and is expected to transform India's healthcare system.

Also, the Indian government has been running a campaign (PMBJPK) that provides medicines at affordable prices.

If implemented properly, these schemes could be a game-changer for the poor.

In July 2018, India's supreme court said that the private hospitals in Delhi, which were allowed to buy land at a concessional rate, should provide free treatment to the poor as per the quota.

Various religious and Dharmic organisations in India are running free hospitals, which also include free expensive treatments like heart surgery or chemotherapy. Additionally, not-for-profit or non-governmental organisations are playing an important role in

3 'Quantifying the financial burden of households' out-of-pocket payments on medicines in India: a repeated cross-sectional analysis of National Sample Survey data, 1994–2014', Sakthivel Selvaraj, Habib Hasan Farooqui, Anup Karan.

India's health care sector by providing subsidised or free medical treatment.

The role of non-governmental organisations in India's healthcare sector is crucial; however, it is still not fully understood.

A report prepared by the Public Health Foundation of India, concluded that 'in-depth and updated information about non-governmental organisations is required to involve them in development programmes' as the 'National statistical authorities have also given a very limited focus to account for this sector in their estimates' (Nimai Das, Role of Non-Governmental Organisations Healthcare Sector of India 2016).

If diseases can be prevented or detected early, public health goals can be reached faster. Traditional Indian practices like Ayurveda and Yoga strongly focus on mental and physical wellbeing, and they are deeply rooted in the concept of preventive healthcare. Ayurvedic medicines and treatments are extremely popular and are readily available in the country.

I do believe that preventive healthcare should be the way forward. There are enough examples which show that spending more money on health does not always guarantee better health.

According to the 2017-18 Journal of AAPI, 'Healthcare in America is more expensive than in any other wealthy nation. In 2016, the average American spent $4,571 on their health – a figure five times higher than the average out-of-pocket spending of other countries in the Organisation for Economic Cooperation and Development (OECD), with no measurable better health. The life expectancy of the average US citizen is 78.8 years, just a fraction ahead of the Czech Republic, where the spending was $236 last year'.

The Bloomberg Health-Efficiency Index is based on the efficiency of healthcare systems in countries as it tracks medical costs and value. For any country which does not want to blindly copy the public health spending of developed nations, the ranking of countries in the Bloomberg Health-Efficiency Index can be an absolute eye-opener.

Though America had one of the highest per-capita spending on health care, the life expectancy of Americans, which is about 79 years, was exceeded by more than 25 countries and territories.

The healthcare system should be rooted in the spirit of the Indian concept of '*Sewa*', not business.

Needless and commission-driven diagnostic studies, surgeries and interventions can be avoided if the medical service providers are adequately trained and have genuine intentions.

The challenges are complex, and India's health care system is multi-layered.

During my interaction with the locals, I discovered that many of them were not even aware of hospitals where free treatment or affordable medicines are available. In a country of more than 1.2 billion people, how easy is it to spread awareness about a newly introduced policy or a scheme?

Providing top-quality health care – and more importantly– encouraging citizens to practice a healthy lifestyle are mandatory duties for any government. Will India succeed in its mission?

SIX

ENVIRONMENT: A GLOBAL PERSPECTIVE

Can Indians clean India?

DO YOU know that the average American produces almost eight times more (7.59) municipal solid waste than the average Indian (World Bank)? Do you know that the average European produces far more e-waste than the average Indian (UNU, 2014)? And do you know that the average Indian also uses fewer plastic materials than the average Westerner?[1]

Still, the West looks shiny and, on the other hand, many Indian streets look dirty. Who is responsible for this mess in India? Citizens or the government? Or both?

1 Source: Plastic Insight - Company Annual Report (2014).

One of India's biggest shortcomings is its poor waste management infrastructure, and the Indian administration is only partly responsible for that.

If you think you are a responsible citizen, give it a thought: Do you segregate your waste? Your country cannot become clean if you don't start doing that. Even a villager in Europe knows how to segregate the waste.

Yes, behavioural changes in people are important but on the other hand, it doesn't mean that the Indian administration cannot learn from European countries how cities can be cleaned even when citizens do not always cooperate.

In many European cities, during weekends, streets tend to become quite dirty in some areas which are next to pubs and football stadiums, sometimes even dirtier than some Indian streets. But in the early hours of Monday morning, European streets are machine cleaned and vacuumed and by the time people wake up to go to the office, they look perfect. I am pretty confident that machines can easily be customised for Indian conditions and roads. But does the Indian administration have the will to bring a paradigm shift that the country needs so desperately?

Yes, India can learn recycling and waste management techniques from the West, but this does not necessarily mean learning western consumption habits.

The municipal solid waste (MSW) can be classified into five main categories.

Where solid waste is properly managed, after the waste is generated, it is segregated at source, then properly stored, collected, transported and treated.

In an effective solid waste management model, there should be a goal to reduce, reuse, recover and recycle waste by using

Main 5 categories of MSW (Municipal solid waste)

1. Recyclable material - glass, bottles, cans, paper, metals, certain plastics, etc.
2. Composite wastes - tetra packs and waste plastics such as toys, waste clothing.
3. Biodegradable waste - paper (can also be recycled), food and kitchen waste, green waste (flowers, vegetables, fruits, leaves).
4. Inert waste - dirt, rocks, construction and demolition waste, debris.
5. Domestic hazardous waste and toxic waste - e-waste, medication, light bulbs, fluorescent tubes, shoe polish, chemicals, paints, batteries, fertilizer and pesticide containers, spray cans.

the appropriate technologies and the waste that is disposed of in landfills should be minimised. Most importantly, landfills should be properly managed so that they don't become a source of greenhouse gases and toxins.

But in many cities of India, the waste that is generated is just recklessly dumped in most cases. Some is dumped on the streets and some is dumped in landfills that are not properly managed and this ends up polluting the air, soil and underground water.

Urban India generates 62 million tonnes of waste (MSW) annually, and it has been predicted that this will reach 165 million tonnes in 2030. As much as 43 million tonnes of municipal solid waste (MSW) is collected annually, out of which 31 million is dumped in landfill sites and just 11.9 million is treated (PIB, Ministry of Environment and Forests, GoI).

There are not enough public bins, and the available bins are not even covered and, in many cases, waste overflows out of those bins and ends up going all over the streets. Waste transporting vehicles are not even covered in many cases which also causes littering of the streets. Many citizens in India recklessly litter the streets too. Probably, they only littered the streets with banana leaves or bowls made of dried leaves a few years earlier. Those kinds of litters were not that harmful as they were biodegradable and could even be eaten by stray animals.

But in India today, what is mostly littered is plastic and, in any society, it's not easy to bring a quick cultural change.

India's informal recycling sector that consists of waste pickers/ *kabadiwalas* plays a crucial role in segregating and recycling waste but in most cases, they are not formally trained and at times they burn wastes at landfills to keep themselves warm at night and end up starting landfill fires that cause air pollution. And because of inadequate gear, they are also exposed to diseases and injuries.

The size of landfills in India is constantly increasing and that is fast becoming a major concern.

Contrary to the composition of waste in western countries, the majority of India's waste is organic (Central Pollution Control Board 2012-13) which means that there is a tremendous opportunity to compost a lot of it. But to make that possible, Indians need to adopt the practice of segregating waste at its source. That is why it is important for Indians to follow the guidelines that are set by the Indian Government in its official solid waste management rules (SWMR).

The SWMR focuses on segregation of waste at its source. All commercial institutions and resident welfare associations are required to partner with the ULB (Urban Local Body) and segregate waste into different categories – biodegradable, non-biodegradable, construction-demolition, domestic-hazardous, horticulture, sanitary, etc.

In addition, they also need to process biodegradable waste through on-site composting and the recyclable waste has to be given to authorized recyclers or waste pickers. If the SWMR is properly implemented and is also adopted by the people, it can simply transform the waste management system in India.

This is a perfect opportunity for all the stakeholders to come on board, get interlinked and benefit from a combination of centralised and decentralised waste management system.

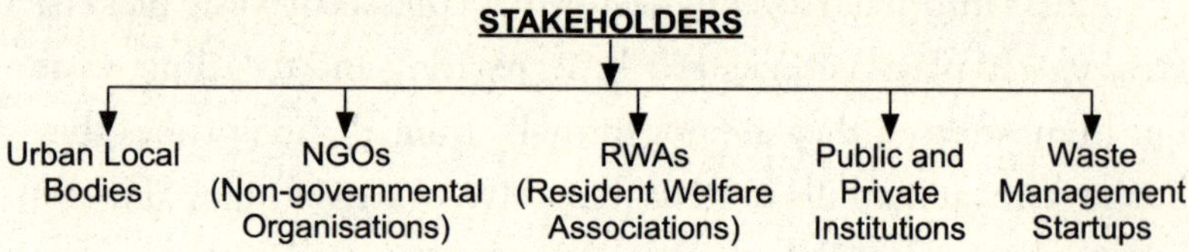

In 2017, India's largest power generation company, NTPC Limited (an Indian Public Sector Undertaking) invited Indian and international developers to build 100 waste to energy projects.

In 2012-13, India had just eight waste-to-energy facilities. Some of the waste-to-energy facilities that were built in the past were not successful (for example: MSW incinerator built at Timarpur, New Delhi).

The scenario is a bit different today. The amount of high-calorific waste is increasing in India and the country is gradually trying to adopt waste segregation at source. These two factors are crucial in running waste to energy projects.

Apart from that, there exist waste-to-energy technologies that can process unsegregated and high moisture-low calorie waste too and that can be very useful for a country like India as in many cases bringing a quick change in people's behaviour is not easy and something needs to be done urgently.

Things can change even faster if Indians can adopt the practice of segregating waste in their homes, stop dumping mixed waste and stop littering. There are many positive stories too. Shanti Niketan housing colony of South Delhi has been composting their waste for quite a while. Gurugram's Regency Park II in DLF Phase 4 is another good example and Tirunelveli in Tamil Nadu became the first city that ensured 100 per cent segregation of solid waste at source.

The citizens of Alappuzha in Kerala had to come up with a decentralised system of composting their biodegradable waste as its municipality does not collect waste because it has no place to dispose it. The story of Alappuzha has now become an inspiration to many other cities of the world after their work was recognised by the UNEP. In urban India, many waste management startups and NGOs are slowly coming up, something that needs to be encouraged.

I have personally visited some villages in Ladakh, Maharashtra, and Jharkhand which were indeed very clean. On the other hand, it is heartbreaking to know that there are villages in India where plastic can enter, but it can never leave. Even though Himachal Pradesh has discouraged the use of plastic shopping bags, plastic still enters the remote isolated villages in Himachal Pradesh in the form of chips packets, water bottles etc. In those areas, there is no mechanism to recycle or collect that plastic trash. There is no service by the administration whatsoever to collect trash from those villages. As a result, many villagers just innocently burn it or dump it in the open.

So, can Indian streets become clean?

Yes, it is possible if Indians start to segregate waste at its source and adopt a decentralised system of composting their biodegradable waste. They can do this by interlinking their RWAs (Resident Welfare Associations), (ULBs) Urban Local Bodies, Non-Governmental Organisations (NGOs) and the private sector.

On the sidelines, informal recycling by waste pickers can be made more organised by training and educating them, as NGOs are doing in Bengaluru, Vellore and Coimbatre. This approach will reduce the burden on India's centralised waste management system which can mostly focus on dealing with the waste that needs sophisticated or large-scale treatment.

By ensuring maximum resource extraction from waste, combined with safe disposal of residual waste through waste to energy projects and through properly managed engineered landfills, India can make its streets clean.

But a shortage of environmental professionals and qualified engineers can totally spoil the plans and that is why it is important that India builds dedicated waste management colleges and universities which will cater for the rising demand of skilled professionals.

Yes, India needs to spend a lot of money to create an efficient waste management infrastructure but a 'clean' India will be able to earn more by attracting more tourists.

A 'clean' India will also save more in its public health care and also it will save money by avoiding those city floods which happen in monsoon due to the drains that are choked by plastic.

Moreover, new jobs will be created, and people will start looking at waste as an opportunity to create wealth.

In 2003, Mawlynnong, a village in Indian State of Meghalaya was declared as the cleanest village in Asia (by *Discover India* magazine). There is no doubt that, in relatively small patches, many streets and districts in India are well maintained and clean too. But these success stories are not enough. India needs a lot more of them and it needs them urgently.

Furthermore, India shouldn't follow the unethical western trend of waste dumping in poorer countries. In 2013, Interpol revealed that one in three containers leaving the European Union contained illegal e-waste which was deceitfully classified as 'used goods' (Interpol).

On multiple occasions, the Philippines President has asked Canada to take back its 100 shipping containers of trash which were sent to Manila in 2013 and 2014 disguised as recyclable material (CTV, Canada).

As India continues to rebuild, its citizens should ensure that they avoid reaching the dangerous levels of an average Westerner in plastic consumption and waste production because waste reduction is better than any kind of waste management. And India's traditional wisdom of 'Aparigraha' which is very relevant even today can play a key role in achieving that.

Air pollution – a global killer

Air pollution causes several million deaths per year globally: 95 per cent of people across the world breath unsafe air, making it a global public health crisis, says Greenpeace, 2018.

Nitrogen dioxide, sulfur dioxide, ground-level ozone, particulate matter (PM2.5, PM10, etc.), carbon monoxide and lead are considered to be the most common air pollutants.

While the developed countries of Europe are known for their dangerously high levels of nitrogen dioxide and ozone, the air of many cities in India is mostly affected by pollution from particulate matter.

The next time you read the sensational and alarming news headlines of the ranking of the world's most polluted cities, you may want to pay attention to the pollutant that is being considered in those rankings. While there are plenty of reports which reveal the rankings for the world's most polluted cities in terms of particulate matter (PM 2.5), in which Indian and Chinese cities usually rank high, for some strange reasons, it is not easy to find the reports or studies which rank the world's most polluted cities in terms of nitrogen dioxide, which is also a dangerous pollutant. Why?

Well, during the last few decades, many European cities have been suffering from extremely hazardous levels of nitrogen-dioxide.

Additionally, it does appear that the western researchers and journalists who love to calculate their countries' GDP on a per capita basis are very hesitant in calculating their country's PM2.5 or nitrogen dioxide emissions on a per capita basis. Why? Is the individual responsibility not important when it comes to environmental protection?

And why do the western journalists not talk about consumption-based emissions more often? Why do they not talk more frequently about historical emissions? Why do they not calculate historical/cumulative emissions in per capita basis? Why do they not discuss individual ecological footprint more frequently? Where will the western nations rank in these calculations? When it comes to historical and individual environmental responsibility for our planet, aren't these indicators more accurate and fairer?

In the northern states of India, the smog is a mixture of stubble (crop residue) burning, construction dust, road dust and vehicular pollution but the biggest contributor is stubble burning by the farmers in Punjab and Haryana (as per an IIT Kanpur study).

The traditional practice of cutting rice manually has slowly discontinued as combine harvesters were introduced in the 1980s. Combine harvesters cut the crop eight inches above the ground; farmers usually get around 15 days for the sowing of wheat; labourers are not readily available and that is why they choose to dispose of the straw by burning it.

There are solutions to this:

Happy Seeder – a zero tillage technology-based tractor-mounted machine that cuts rice straw and sows wheat into the soil is an option. A survey which was done by Ridhima Gupta (Agro-environmental revolution in Punjab: Case of the happy seeder technology) and another case study which was done by IGS, Bihar (Case Study on Zero Tillage Technique, CUTS International) supported the idea of zero tillage technology in farming that can yield more profits and does not require farmers to burn the crop residue. Farm machinery like the happy seeder, chopper-shredder and rotavator can be provided to farmers at a subsidised price, number of biomass plants can also be increased (Punjab Pollution Control Board-2017) with a transparent and efficient system of payments to farmers. However, the tariff of the electricity generated from such power plants remains a very important factor.

In addition, farmers can be encouraged to grow basmati rice; not only is the Basmati variety sold for a higher price, it also requires manual harvesting. Use of paddy straw in producing paper, card boards, packing materials can be encouraged and it can also be used as biomass pellet fuel (in an industrial boiler).

If labourers are available, farmers can also learn the technique of incorporating the straw back into the soil as it can improve the fertility of the soil and money can then be saved on fertilisers.

And yes, farmers do need to be educated so that they are able to comfortably switch to the new farming techniques. This will also protect their own health as rural Punjab spends around USD 1.1 million (7.6 cr) in medical bills due to crop residue burning.[2]

2 Valuing the Health Effects of Air Pollution from Agricultural Residue Burning, Pramod Kumar, Surender Kumar.

Inefficient traffic management and badly planned Indian roads lead to traffic jams and vehicular pollution, even though the greater percentage of Indians go to work using their private vehicles, which is not as high as in many western nations (Census 2011, EEA, Who Drives to Work? Commuting by Automobile in the United States: 2013, Brian McKenzie).

India's poorly managed construction sites are also a source of particulate matter. Mechanised road cleaning by vacuuming is almost non-existent; however, one can easily spot old-style manual sweeping everywhere, which disperses a lot of dust in the air.

India's unique geography, its weather conditions and wind patterns, its unpaved roads that disperse dust, unofficial burning of trash by random individuals, are some of the other contributing factors to this smog.

The dust control measures by the National Green Tribunalare not properly implemented and followed, whether it is real estate developers or private individuals. In a 2018 report by Greenpeace, high levels of NO2 air pollution were noticed in three Indian cities.

On the other hand, the good news is that India has been continually increasing its per centage of energy that is produced by renewable sources. According to a report from NITI Aayog, India will be able to reduce its projected carbon emissions by 37 per cent by 2030, if it can adopt the use of electric vehicles and more public transportation.

To tackle air pollution in Delhi, there is also an action plan, which is called GRAP (Graded Response Action Plan). It received approval (from the nodal Environment Pollution Control Authority/Oct 18, 2017) and it requires a serious implementation.

While countries like India appear more concerned about the particulate matter related pollution, western countries are struggling from pollution from gases like nitrogen dioxide and ozone.

NO_2, and NO_x more generally, cause lung damage and respiratory symptoms from acute exposure. In long-term exposure, it increases the risk of chronic diseases (Greenpeace).

The 2013 EEA report revealed that more than 90 per cent of people in European cities were breathing dangerous air (Air quality in Europe – 2013 report, EEA).

Are you familiar with the 2014 research by London's King's College, which revealed that the famous Oxford Street of London was the most polluted street in the world with 463 micrograms of nitrogen dioxide per cubic meter of air? The most horrifying thing about nitrogen dioxide is that it is not visible like Delhi's smog. So, you may have a blue sky, but you are breathing in toxic air.

David Carslaw of King's College said that 'NO_2 concentrations (in Oxford Street) are as high as they ever have been in the long history of air pollution'.

In 2017, the analysis commissioned by its Labour government revealed that nearly 40 million people in the UK are living in illegal limits of nitrogen dioxide pollution.

And 63 per cent of the most sensitive wildlife habitats in the UK are affected by excessive nitrogen deposits (We need talk about nitrogen, *Plant Link* UK).

It is not just the UK, which is suffering from pollution due to nitrogen dioxide, the invisible killer is all over Europe and also in many cities of the US(EEA).

In addition, ozone pollution is a major concern in many European countries (EEA).

And here is another perspective. It is the image that was released by NASA in which heavy concentrations of nitrogen dioxide can be seen in Europe.

This global map shows the concentration of nitrogen dioxide in the troposphere as detected by the Ozone Monitoring Instrument aboard the Aura satellite, averaged over 2014.

It is absolutely astonishing to see how some of these European countries with their tiny population can manage to produce so much nitrogen dioxide. It is quite scary to even imagine what their nitrogen dioxide emissions in per capita terms would be. Not to mention that a few years ago, the situation in Europe was even worse.

On 11 September 2018, the official website of The European Court of Auditors reported:

> EU action to protect human health from air pollution has not delivered its expected impact, according to a new report from the European Court of Auditors. Every year, air pollution causes about 400,000 premature deaths in the EU and hundreds of billions of euros in health-related external costs. However, these significant human and economic costs have not yet been reflected in adequate action across the Union, warn the auditors. They add that particulate matter, nitrogen dioxide and ground level ozone are the air pollutants responsible for most of the early deaths and that people in urban areas are particularly exposed.

EU air quality standards, which were established 20 years ago are still not uniformly adopted by all member states. Air, which can be classified as 'sufficient' in Krakow or Sofia, is actually considered 'very poor' by EEA standards. What is considered 'fair' in Ostrava and 'mediocre' in Milan is classified as 'poor' by EEA standards and what makes matters worse is that even EEA standards fall short of those recommended by the WHO.

Air pollution-related warnings have been issued to international tourists who travel to New Delhi, but have you ever heard of global warnings that are issued to tourists who visit London's Oxford Street, or its other nitrogen dioxide-filled cities?

Yes, tourists should be warned when they are visiting Delhi on those days when air pollution is peaking, but why are such warnings not issued to innocent international tourists who are visiting London and other European cities too? These cities also have dangerously high levels of nitrogen dioxide; especially an important city like London, which gets a lot more international tourists than Delhi – their lives and health are at risk.

Is it just because the naked eye can't see the nitrogen dioxide of London, just the way it can see smog in Delhi or is it because everybody can shame Delhi, but nobody can shame London?

And the same goes for other nitrogen dioxide filled cities of France, Germany or Italy or other European cities.

Nitrogen dioxide causes thousands of premature deaths in Europe:

Death numbers are even worse when pollutants like particulates and ozone are also taken into account. Before Brexit in 2014, in just 28 countries of the European Union, more than half a million (502,351) premature deaths were linked with air pollution and Germany had the highest number. (Source: EEA, 2014).

PM_{10} air quality indices (as of March 2018)

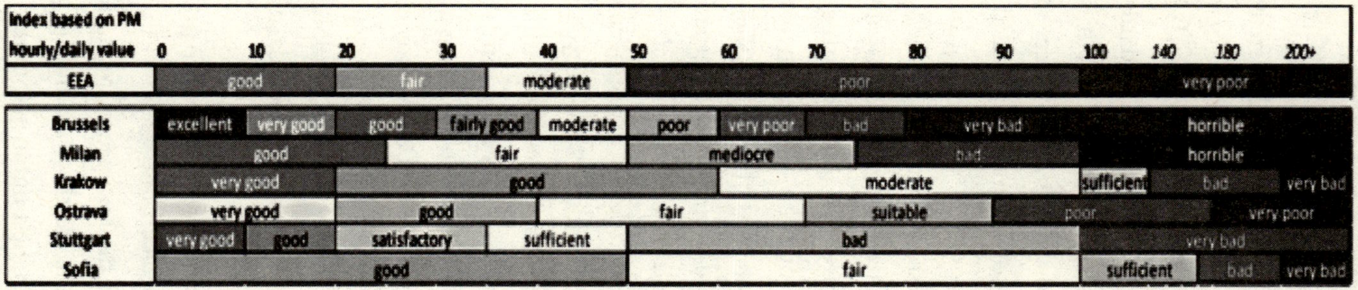

Source: EEA and cities website.

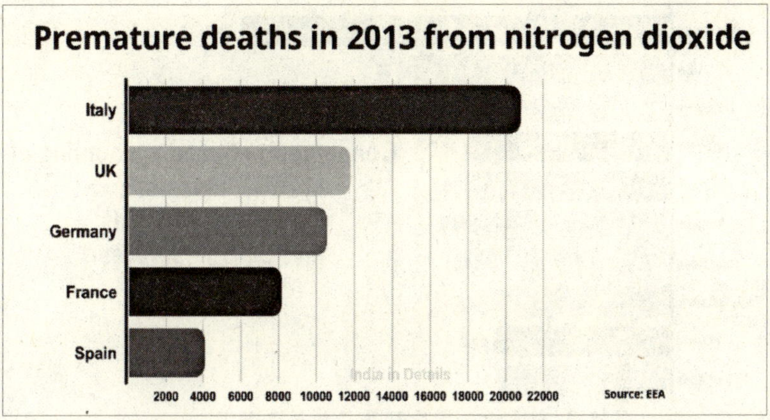

Source: EEA

Emissions in the atmosphere easily last for centuries and it is totally fair to hold the countries responsible for climate change by calculating their historical / cumulative emissions.

It is absolutely shocking to learn that almost 80 per cent of our planet's historical emissions have come from Europe and the USA. (World Resources Institute).

It is shocking to see that many of these western countries have caused massive damage to our planet from their massive historical emissions, and they continue to emit a lot more emissions than countries like India. A recent report revealed that Canada's vehicles have the highest average carbon dioxide emissions and fuel consumption per kilometre driven. Not only that, the vehicles in Canada are also the largest and the second heaviest in the world. The second rank is held by the USA (International Energy Agency, 2019).

In addition, many western countries have cleverly outsourced their emissions by moving their pollution-causing factories to poorer countries, which is why it is very important to understand consumption-based emissions.

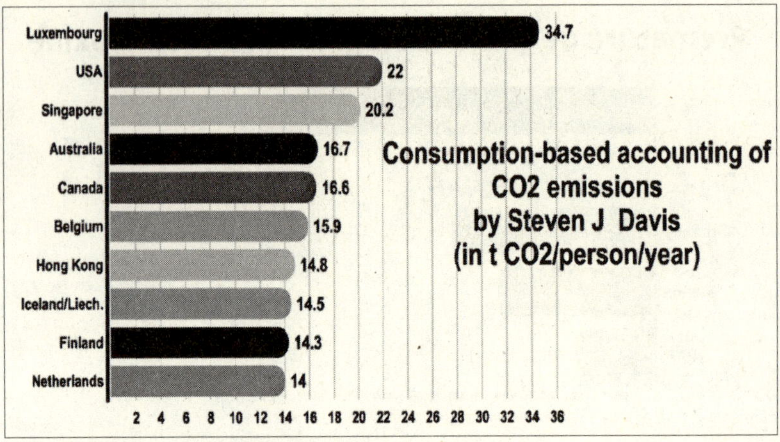

The calculation of emissions, which is based on consumption instead of production, is a great way to hold those countries responsible which consume goods that cause emissions elsewhere.

To understand individual responsibility, consumption-based emissions should be calculated on per capita terms.

India looks after more than 18 per cent of the world's population with just 2.4 per cent of land area and only 4 per cent of renewable water resources. As such, India has to look at its own situation of ecological reserves so that it does not face a situation of ecological deficit.

Our planet is our common asset and we all should carry equal responsibility. If you are from the West, and if you care about the environment, start calculating and reducing your ecological footprint; because if everyone in the developing and poor countries adopt the lifestyle of an average American or an average European, we will need a few Earths (Global footprint network).

Just because one is born in America or in Europe, one does not get the inherent right to consume more and emit more than an average Indian.

So, isn't it all about consumerism in the end? Isn't it all about the fact that countries around the world have been adopting the western growth model which is based on consumerism? It does look like the root cause of our environmental problems.

But is it possible to have human prosperity while living a sustainable life and by shunning consumerism? Perhaps, the answer to that is hidden somewhere in ancient India, something that I will explore in the next part of this chapter.

Can aparigraha offer a solution to environmental problems?

Work, earn and spend. Fundamentally, the western growth model is based on consumerism. Across the world, many countries have adopted this. Did you know that if everyone in the world started to live like an average American, we would need five Earths? (Global Footprint Network).

The US is the biggest carbon polluter in history and in per capita terms, the results can be even more embarrassing for many western countries. An average Westerner consumes a lot of energy, a lot of water, and a lot of plastic.

It is well established that a meat-based diet is very harsh to the environment. Western nations consume a lot more meat and they also have a very high rate of food wastage.

Many western nations have extremely high historical emissions. Despite this, the average Westerner also produces a lot more e-waste, a lot more municipal solid waste and causes a lot more emissions than an average Indian. An average Westerner lives a lifestyle, which has a very devastating ecological footprint.

Western countries have been unethically dumping their e-waste in Africa and other developing countries.

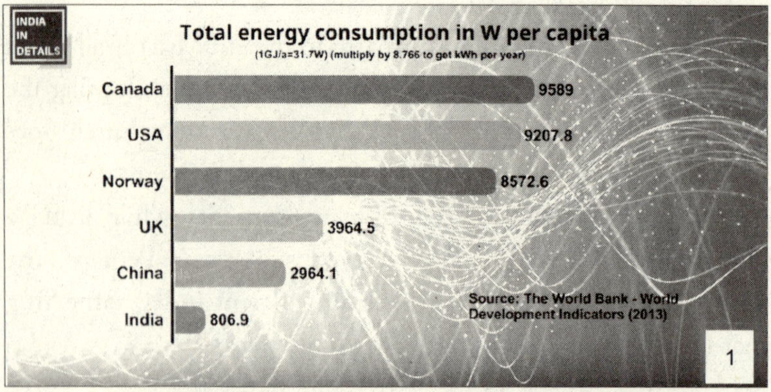

The World Bank – World Development Indicators (2013)

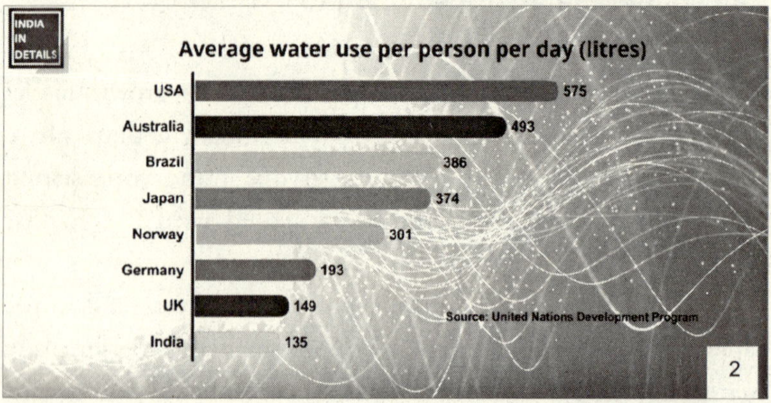

Source: United Nations Development Programme

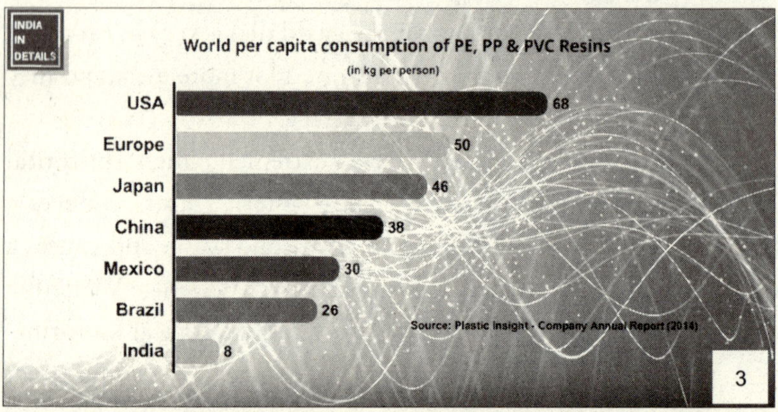

Source: Plastic Insight – Company Annual Report (2014)

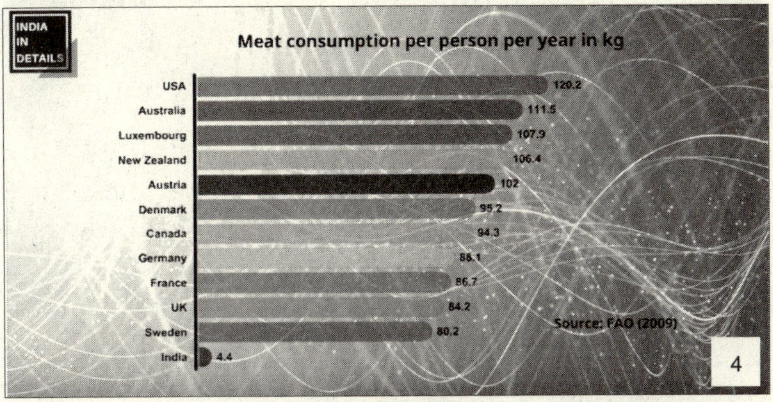

Source: FAO (2009)

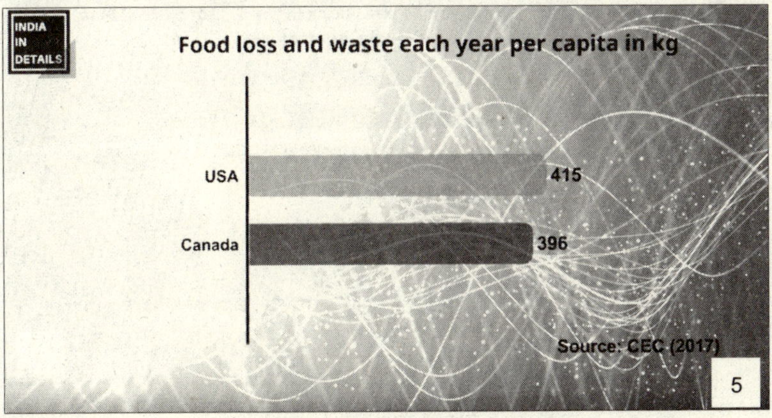

Source: CEC (2017)

Up to 1.3 million tonnes of used electrical products are shipped out of the European Union, which is mostly sent to West Africa and Asia (EEA).

Moreover, many western countries consume goods that cause emissions elsewhere and that is why it is extremely crucial to look at consumption-based emissions (as shown in image on pg 90).

The ecological footprint comparison clearly shows that in terms of environmental damage, an average Indian is nowhere

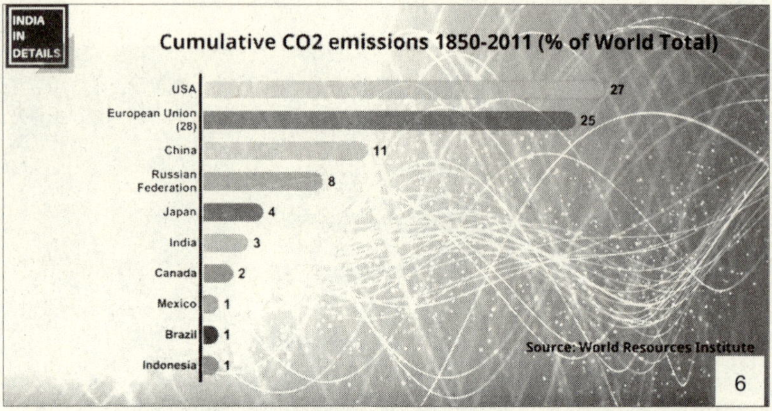

Source: World Resources Institute

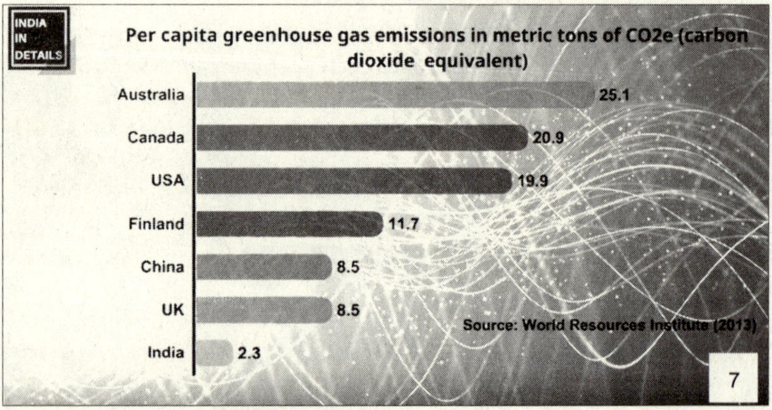

Source: World Resources Instutue (2013)

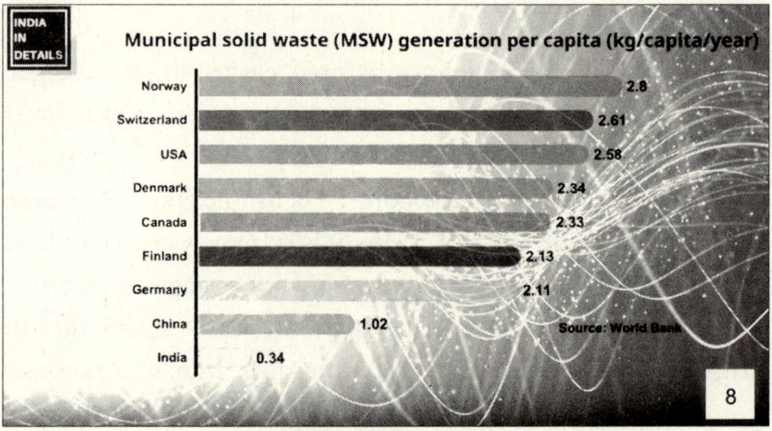

Source: World Bank

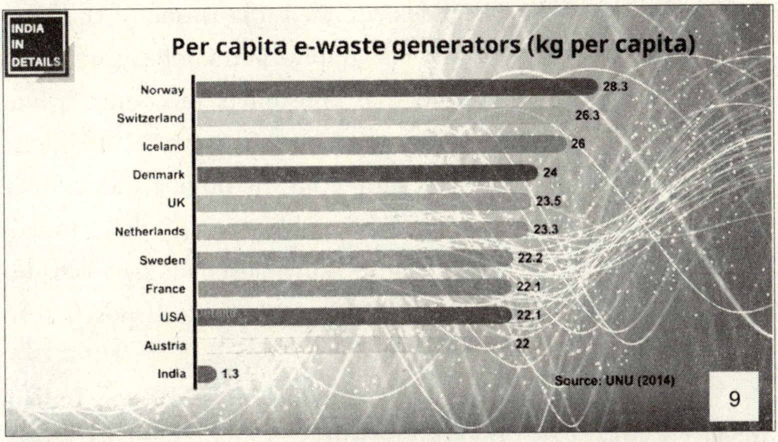

Source: UNU (2014)

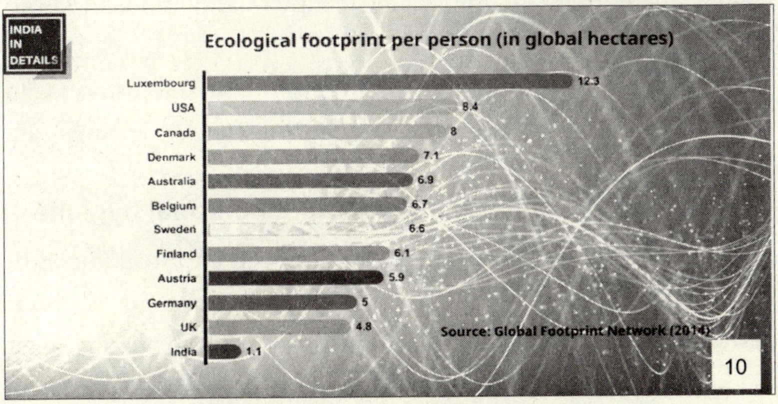

Source: Global Footprint Network (2014)

close to an average Westerner, whose ecological footprint is many times higher (as shown in Picture 10).

The average US household has 300,000 things. American children make up 3.7 per cent of children on the planet but have 47 per cent of all the toys and children's books.[3]

3 Source: (Statistics cited by Regina Lark, professional organiser).

According to the Greendex survey, India is one of the least wasteful economies (National Geographic and GlobeScan).

This survey also revealed that consumers in countries like Sweden, Britain and Germany had been the worst offenders, but still they express the least guilt. On the other hand, Indian consumers live the most sustainable lifestyle. Modern India's recycling system is a witness to how sustainability can be supported. In spite of that, Indian consumers feel most guilty about their impact on the environment.

While this all sounds pretty favourable, but still, many Indian and rivers look dirty. Why? It is because of India's inefficient waste management (refer to the related chapter) and India needs to work on that.

Can India take inspiration from its own past and history? Can India make the most of its timeless traditional knowledge? Yes, it can.

Sustainability – water, conservation, personal hygiene

In India, the concept of Aparigraha has been an integral part of Dharmic societies for thousands of years. Aparigraha is about non-possessiveness and self-discipline, which means taking what is absolutely necessary.

Many Dharmic scriptures highlight the importance of preserving the environment, wildlife conservation and of personal hygiene. A few examples are from Dharmic scriptures: *Isha Upnishada, Charaka Samhita* and *Susruta Samhita* (Sanskrit text on Ayurveda).

More than two thousand years ago, Emperor Ashoka made deforestation and the killing of various species of animals illegal by getting edicts inscribed on iron pillars and rocks throughout his kingdom.

There are multiple examples of water conservation in India's history and traditions.

Some randomly chosen examples of
water conservation in india's history and traditions

- Nagaland: Zabo system
- Tamil Nadu: *Eri*
- Andhra pradesh: *Cheruvu*
- Karnataka: *Keres*
- Gujarat: *Rani ki Vav* etc.
- Rajasthan: *Baoli, Nadi, jhalara, Taanka, Bandhi, Bawari, Khadin, Chauka system*
- North india: *Traditional water conservation by johad*
- North East india: *Bamboo Drip irrigation, Dongs*
- Bihar: *Ahar Pynes*
- Kerala: *Panam keni*
- Maharashtra: P*had system, Ramtek Model*
- Ladakh: *Zing system*
- Himachal Pradesh: *Kuhls*
- Madhya Pradesh: *Pat System*
- Great Nicobar Islands: *Jackwells*

In Dharmic traditions, divinity exists everywhere. The great sacrifices of Bishnoi community are very well known and their heroic acts have inspired many movements like Chipko and Appiko.

Bhil tribes of Madhya Pradesh's Jhabua and Alirajpur districts are using their age-old tradition 'halma' to conserve environment.

India's Ayurveda focuses on preventive health care and it encourages a vegetarian diet. It recommends the consumption of seasonal fruits and vegetables that are grown locally. Such practices save energy that is consumed in transportation.

India's traditional system is all about reducing, reusing and recycling.

In traditional Indian cuisine, leftovers are used to make mouth-watering nutritious dishes. The curd rice of South India, Dal Paratha of North India, Khakra of Gujarat are a few examples.

Sun drying is used to preserve food and in Indian kitchens,

using cloth instead of paper towels is a common traditional practice. Reusing old clothes to make new handbags or making new fabric of Khadi that uses very little water, traditional Indian system has always been very gentle on nature.

In many ancient Indian temples, mortar was hardly used as the stones were attached using a special technique that involved gravity.

Yes, it is true that the traditional Indian system is full of such evidences and examples but India is witnessing rapid urbanisation. Will India be able to preserve its traditional knowledge?

Will India be able to achieve prosperity through greener ways and will it be able to empower those at the bottom of the pyramid?

My search for these answers encouraged me to take a short drive from Mumbai that brought me to the Govardhan Ecovillage (GEV), which is located in the foothills of the Sahyadhri Mountains.

Govardhan Ecovillage is located in one of the most backward regions of India and it has been working on sustainable rural development and eco-tourism for many years.

Press Information Bureau
Government of India
Ministry of Commerce & Industry

30-January-2018 18:21 IST

"Taking Khadi: local to Global"

Discussion at Indian Institute of Foreign Trade

Textiles and apparel sector has made a significant contribution by providing both direct and indirect employment to almost 35 and 50million Indians respectively, making it the largest employment sector after agriculture. This makes Khadi an important segment for concentrating towards export promotion.A round table discussion on taking KHADI:local to global was organized by Indian Institute of Foreign Trade on 30th Jan 2018 with support from KVIC and UDAANSKILL. The event focused on connecting the global demand and supply of Khadi, identifying newer markets and product diversification; developing promotional strategies to enter newer markets, inputs on trade policy, market access at WTO front, compliances, design interventions and possibilities of CSR interventions from corporates and PSUs....

Shri. V.K.Saxena, Chairman, KHADI AND Village Industries Commission who was the Guest of honour explained about the diversity of efforts made by KVIC towards promotion of Khadi right from meeting the issues on raw material procurement, wage levels of rural artisans, technological and design interventions and making it a sustainable and export worthy segment. *"Its export worthiness also comes from the fact that Indian Khadi earns a lot of water and carbon foot print since it requires only 3 litres of water as compared to 56 liters in other fabrics"* said Mr. Saxena.

By providing education, organising skill development programmes and adopting various rural-specific alternative sources, it has encouraged sustainable development of the local tribal communities.

It has been providing free school lunches to thousands of children, conducting health camps and empowering tribal women by encouraging micro enterprise creation.

It has provided organic farming training to hundreds of farmers and it has successfully transformed a wasteland into a cultivable vegetable garden using smart agricultural innovation.

GEV's symbiotic waste recycling system caught my attention. Kitchen and cattle waste is used in a biogas plant and as a natural fertilizer, plastic and cement bags are utilised to store compost, mud and food waste. Construction waste is utilised in making permanent raised beds for farming and human waste is treated in the soil Biotechnology plant.

In GEV, the output of one system becomes the input of another system.

Today, India is full of construction sites. It is estimated that the construction sector in India emits about 22 per cent of India's total annual CO2 emissions (Development Alternatives).

In times such as these, GEV's implementation of green building technologies and its smart management of construction waste is very inspiring.

By local procurement and by using low embodied energy housing materials, it has succeeded in reducing its ecological footprint.

Its smart approach in alternative energies and its water resource development in rural areas has helped in creating a community that lives in harmony with nature.

India's traditional knowledge is not only helping sustainable projects like GEV but also inspiring many Westerners.

The Leaf Republic of Germany is a good example. It is selling biodegradable plates (imported from India) that are made of dried leaves. In many parts of India, these plates are known as 'Pattal' and eating in them is just a normal traditional practice.

India is aiming to become a USD 10 trillion economy by 2030 (Nominal GDP) and it wants to reach that milestone in a greener way.

It has already taken giant steps in solar energy and it is on track to meet 2030 Nationally Determined Contribution targets.

Far away from London's polluted air, which is filled with Nitrogen dioxide, and far away from particulate matter-filled streets of Delhi... for many visitors, breathing the fresh air of GEV was almost a luxury, something that I experienced during my stay.

Our planet does not need more environmental activists, it just needs more individuals with a low ecological footprint.

We are living in critical times. Sea creatures are eating plastic in our oceans and most of us are unaware that even our tap water is contaminated by plastic particles (ORB Media).

An average citizen of many western countries actively participates in the system that dumps e-waste in other countries and outsources emissions to other countries. This is not a solution. According to a UN Environment Programme (UNEP) research, 60-90 per cent of e-waste worth 19 billion dollars is illegally dumped or traded. We help the system run by consuming goods that hurt humans, animals and nature before they reach us. Yes, we are involved. We are the very backbone of the economy that is based the work-earn-spend model.

As long as we are greedy, self-indulgent and self-serving, there will never be a true environmental revolution.

An inner revolution is needed to bring about an environmental revolution and that is why, India's traditional knowledge is deeply interlinked with spirituality and inner well-being.

Yes, it is possible to prosper without hurting our planet. Yes, it is possible to keep the soul of India's villages alive. Through the use of India's traditional knowledge, GEV has successfully demonstrated that.

A lesser-known fact: 327 million Americans own 163 million cats and dogs. This has a massive carbon footprint as much of the food of dogs and cats is meat.

Meat production is also known for its contribution to climate change (Shifting Diets for a Sustainable Food Future, World Resources Institute, Exploring the biophysical option space for feeding the world without deforestation, Karl-Heinz Erb, Christian Lauk, Thomas Kastner, Andreas Mayer, Michaela C Theurl & Helmut Haberl).

If American pet cats and dogs had their own country, it would be the fifth in the world for its consumption of meat (Okin's study).

In comparison, 1.3 billion Indians have 10 million pets (India International Pet Trade Fair).

Should Indians also go the 'American way'?

SEVEN

INDIA'S GLOBAL FIGHT AGAINST HUNGER AND POVERTY

IN INDIA, 21 per cent of children aged under five suffer from wasting, which means that their weight is too low for their height.

As many as 38 per cent of children aged under five are stunted, which means that their height is too short for their age. (Source: NFHS-4).

Between 2014 and 2016, 15.2 per cent of the population in India was undernourished.

During the same period, 9.3 per cent of the population was undernourished in China (FAO).

Child and maternal undernutrition is the main cause of death of children under five years of age (*The Lancet*, 2013) and it is well-known that malnourished children have a higher risk of death from malaria, pneumonia and diarrhea.

The launch of the National Nutrition Mission (NNM) is expected to improve the overall situation in India and it needs to be properly implemented. (Source: PIB).

During my investigations, I discovered a charitable organisation called Akshaya Patra, which has already served more than three billion meals in India. The organisation is headquartered in Bengaluru and has done exceptionally well in its attempt to eliminate classroom hunger through the Mid-Day Meal Scheme.

The organisation began its journey by feeding 1500 school children in five schools of Bengaluru and today, it is providing free food in nearly 14,000 schools in the country.

Akshaya Patra's meals have also helped in improving enrolment and attendance and their aim is to serve five million children by 2020.

The foundation has been investing in various green initiatives, which is also helping them in cost reduction.

Akshaya Patra may be a charitable organisation, but they have a very corporate approach, headed by an IITian. Good hygiene practices, proper monitoring and documentation make them more efficient and less prone to accidents.

Akshaya Patra is not only serving the children of India but it has also started to serve nutritious vegetarian meals to students and the homeless in different parts of London.

There are 500,000 children in the UK who go to school hungry, according to the Felix Project Year-2017. And, out of these 500,000 children, 70,000 are in London city.

It is estimated that nearly one third of the food produced in the world for human consumption every year gets lost or wasted, according to the FAO.

But food alone may not be enough to fight undernutrition and that is why we need a holistic approach that takes account of nutritional disorders, immunisation, safe drinking water, sanitation and hygiene. Dedicated behavioural counseling can help in preventing and managing infections.

India is home to the largest number of children in the world and nearly every fifth child in the world lives in India.

India's children will secure India's future and India needs to protect them.

The journey to prosperity can be shortened if India can successfully reach out to those at the bottom of the pyramid.

Akshaya Patra's significant contributions in the global fight against hunger and its success story should inspire future generations. The scale and capacity may be different, but on a positive note, there are plenty of other organisations in India that are doing similar work. India's fight against hunger and poverty is truly global in every sense. Chapter 2 highlights how the overseas Indians are also continuing this mission.

EIGHT

A GLOBAL PERSPECTIVE ON SEXUAL CRIMES

GLOBALLY, WOMEN and children are facing violence. Can we afford to live in denial? Can we afford to shame other nations by indulging in mud-slinging and not look within our own country to fight this global menace? As a concerned global citizen, I feel that a broader global perspective is absolutely required as it will enable us to study the corrupt human behaviour more comprehensively. Only when we are fully informed about the problem globally, we will be able to find an effective solution.

As many as 27 per cent of Europeans think that rape may be acceptable in some circumstances, says the Special Eurobarometer 449-November 2016, Gender-based violence.

In the USA, nearly one in five women has been a victim of rape or attempted rape, according to CDC.

In Europe (across the 28 Member States of the European Union), 10 per cent of women have experienced some form of sexual violence since the age of 15, says the The European Union Agency for Fundamental Rights.

Just within France, about four million women (12 per cent of the total) have been raped at least once in their lives (Fondation Jean Jaurès).

Nearly 42 million people in the United States are living with a history of sexual abuse during childhood (Darkness to Light, USA).

These numbers are frightening but what is even more frightening is that most of these crimes go unreported.

It was estimated by The National Crime Agency (UK) that 750,000 men in Britain have an interest in having sex with children.

According to Theresa May, child sex abuse is 'woven, covertly, into the fabric' of British society.[1]

In terms of rape rate, this is how these countries (randomly chosen) stand:

- Iceland 55.32
- England and Wales 36.44
- USA* 35.85
- New Zealand 32.05
- Scotland* 31.72
- Belgium 29.99
- France* 17.5
- India 2.63

---

1 https://www.telegraph.co.uk/news/2016/08/05/child-abuse-in-the-uk-runs-far-deeper-than-you-know/

- Canada* (2012) 1.43

(Source: UNODC, Rape Rate per 100,000 population in 2013).

*Changes in definitions and/or counting rules are reported by the Member State to indicate a break in the time series.

But, this doesn't tell the whole story. Under-reporting is one of the main factors and it shouldn't be overlooked.

According to FRA survey 2014, in Europe:

- As many as 33 per cent of women have experienced physical and/or sexual violence since the age of 15. That corresponds to 62 million women.
- 22 per cent have experienced physical and/or sexual violence by a partner.
- 5 per cent of all women have been raped. Almost one in 10 women who have experienced sexual violence by a non-partner, indicate that more than one perpetrator was involved in the most serious incident.
- 43 per cent have experienced some form of psychological violence by either a current or a previous partner, such as public humiliation; forbidding a woman to leave the house or locking her up; forcing her to watch pornography; and threats of violence.
- 33 per cent have childhood experiences of physical or sexual violence at the hands of an adult. 12 per cent had childhood experiences of sexual violence, of which half were from men they did not know. These forms of abuse typically involve an adult exposing their genitals or touching the child's genitals or breasts.
- 18 per cent of women have experienced stalking since the age of 15 and 5 per cent in the 12 months prior to the

interview. This corresponds to 9 million women. 21 per cent of women who have experienced stalking said that it lasted for over 2 years.

- 11 per cent of women have experienced inappropriate advances on social websites or have been subjected to sexually explicit emails or text (SMS) messages. 20 per cent of young women (18-29) have been victims of such cyberharassment.
- 55 per cent of women have experienced some form of sexual harassment. 32 per cent of all victims of sexual harassment said the perpetrator was a boss, colleague or customer.
- 67 per cent did not report the most serious incident of partner violence to the police or any other organisation."

The Police

Underreporting

For instance, 91 per cent of sexual assaults go unreported in Canada (the 2004 General Social Survey on Victimisation).

In the UK, 85 per cent of those who experience sexual violence do not report to the police.[2]

And when they do end-up contacting the police, the police let them down. A report revealed that in the UK, the under-recording rate for victims of sexual offences is 26 per cent.

In the USA, figures by the Department of Justice confirm massive underreporting of rape. Additionally, the data from

2 An Overview of Sexual Offending in England and Wales, Ministry of Justice, Home Office & the Office for National Statistics, 2013.

Crime-recording: making the victim count

The final report of an inspection of crime data integrity in police forces in England and Wales

November 2014

ISBN: 978-1-78246-660-4

HMIC Inspecting policing in the public interest

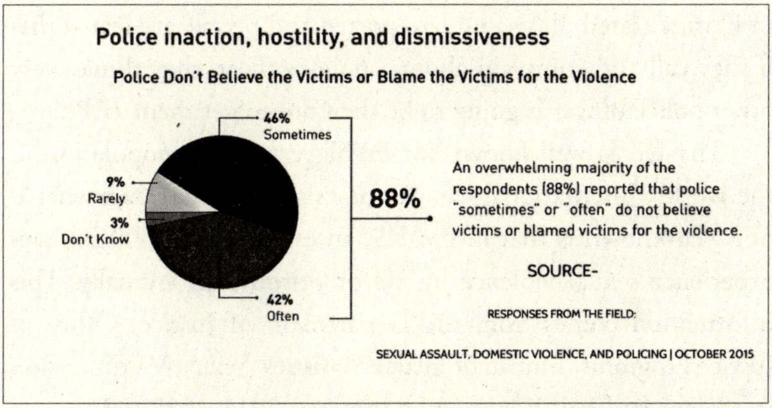

Source: Responses from the Field: Sexual Assault, Domestic Violence, and Policing | October 2015

Centers for Disease Control and Prevention (CDC,2015) indicates that more than 90 per cent of rapes go unreported.

Police misbehaviour

Not just that, police in the US do not believe the victims and even blame the victims for the violence.

American Police officers themselves commit a lot of crimes. The

Cato Institute's National Police Misconduct Reporting Project, 2010 Annual Report revealed that sexual assault rates are significantly higher for police when compared to the general population.

An Associated Press investigation revealed that American police officers were involved in very serious crimes such as: possession of child abuse images, rape, sodomy and other sexual assault, sexual misconduct, such as propositioning citizens or having consensual but prohibited on-duty intercourse.

People fear the police and that is why police crime in the US is very underreported.

Chief Bernadette DiPino of the Sarasota Police Department in Florida stated: 'It's so underreported and people are scared that if they call and complain about a police officer, they think every other police officer is going to be then out to get them' (AP).

The US is well known for its biggest prison population in the world (International Centre for Prison Studies), but what is not well-known is that in the US, an estimated 80,600 inmates experience sexual violence by jail or prison staff annually. This information comes from the Department of Justice, Office of Justice Programs, Bureau of Justice Statistics, Sexual Victimization in Prisons and Jails Reported by Inmates, 2011-2012 (2013).

In India, all cases of sexual violence are not reported either.

Of all women in India who have ever experienced any type of sexual violence, only 10 per cent have sought help, says the National Family Health Survey (NFHS-4).

Age of consent

The age of consent is also very important. Below is the definition of rape in the Indian Penal Code. It says: 'With or without her consent, when she is under eighteen years of age'.

> (As of Amendment 2013)
> §375. A man is said to commit 'rape' if he:
> (a) penetrates his penis, to any extent, into the vagina, mouth, urethra or anus of a woman or makes her to do so with him or any other person; or (b) inserts, to any extent, any object or a part of the body, not being the penis, into the vagina, the urethra or anus of a woman or makes her to do so with him or any other person; or (c) manipulates any part of the body of a woman so as to cause penetration into the vagina, urethra, anus or any part of body of such woman or makes her to do so with him or any other person; or (d) applies his mouth to the vagina, anus, urethra of a woman or makes her to do so with him or any other person, under the circumstances falling under any of the following seven descriptions:
> Firstly. — Against her will.
> Secondly. — Without her consent.
> Thirdly. — With her consent, when her consent has been obtained by putting her or any person in whom she is interested, in fear of death or of hurt.
> Fourthly. — With her consent, when the man knows that he is not her husband and that her consent is given because she believes that he is another man to whom she is or believes herself to be lawfully married.
> Fifthly. — With her consent when, at the time of giving such consent, by reason of unsoundness of mind or intoxication or the administration by him personally or through another of any stupefying or unwholesome Substance, she is unable to understand the nature and consequences of that to which she gives consent.
> Sixthly. — With or without her consent, when she is under eighteen years of age.
> Seventhly. — When she is unable to communicate consent…

But, in many European countries, the age of consent is 14.

It was revealed that half of all UK teenagers have their first sexual experience by the age of 14 (National Survey of Sexual Attitudes and Lifestyles).

In France, sex with a child is rape only if prosecutors can prove that it is non-consensual. Recently, a 29-year old man was not charged for rape after having sex with a girl who was 11. In France, the age of consent is set at 15, but the country does not have any law which defines sex with someone below a fixed age as rape.[3]

On the other hand, India allows capital punishment for anyone convicted of raping children under the age of 12.

Indian criminal justice system appears to be far stronger when one takes a closer look at what is happening in many western nations.

For example, in 2016, the Canadian supreme court ruled that sex with animals which involves penetration is a crime, not oral sex. The offender was acquitted of the offence of bestiality.

The offender 'smeared peanut butter on his stepdaughter's vagina to entice the family dog to lick it off... before sexually assaulting the victims he sometimes showed them pornography that involved vaginal sex between humans and animals. He inserted the name of the family dog into the text of pornographic stories he read to the victims prior to the sexually assaulting them, and he kept images of bestiality (in addition to the bestiality images he recorded himself) on his laptop'.[4]

It should also be noted that the Canadian justice system has

---

3 https://www.theguardian.com/world/2018/feb/14/french-girl-11-not-a-child-say-lawyers-for-man-29-accused-of-sexual-abuse

4 'Bestiality' as reflected in Canadian case law Considerations for protecting children and animals after R v DLW 2018 CanLIIDocs 266 Canadian Centre for Child Protection Inc. December 2018.

been criticised for freeing many child murderers, serial killers, mass shooters, cop killers and cannibals.[5]

Marital rape in India and sexual violence by intimate partner in the West

As many as 6.6 per cent of women in India have faced sexual violence from their husband at least once in their lives (NFHS-4). And about 1 per cent of women face it often.

In India, the PWDVA[6] recognises marital rape and provides a definition of domestic violence that is comprehensive and includes all forms of physical, emotional, verbal, sexual, and economic violence, and covers both actual acts of such violence and threats of violence. Under IPC, sexual intercourse by a husband without the wife's express consent is an exception and section 498-A deals in Cruelty by Husbands and Relatives.

In many western societies, marriage is increasingly becoming an outdated concept and that is why one should look at the statistics of 'sexual violence by an intimate partner' to understand the situation better.

It was revealed that almost one-third of American girls who have been in a relationship (29 per cent) were pressured to have sex or to engage in sexual acts when they didn't want to do so (Teen Relationship Abuse Survey).

In Europe (across the 28 Member States of the European Union) one in 10 women has experienced some form of sexual

---

5 https://nationalpost.com/news/canada/here-is-just-a-partial-list-of-the-brutal-murderers-that-canada-has-set-free

6 Protection of Women from Domestic Violence Act 2005.

violence since the age of 15, says the European Union Agency for Fundamental Rights.

Underreporting is a major problem in Europe as it was also revealed that (across the 28 Member States of the European Union) in more than 85 per cent of cases, the most serious incident of partner violence was not reported to the police.

In the UK, 41 per cent of girls 'aged 14 to 17 who reported an intimate relationship experienced some form of sexual violence from their partner', reports the Connect Centre for International Research on Interpersonal Violence and Harm, University of Central Lancashire.

In America it was found that lesbians (and gay men) experience equal or higher rates of partner violence than those who are identified as straight, according to the first national survey of intimate partner violence, USA.

It is also important to highlight the prevailing mindset in many western nations that many may find extremely disturbing:

A total of 31 per cent Lithuanians think that ' forcing a partner to have sex should not be against the law (31 per cent), followed by 24 per cent in the Czech Republic, 21 per cent in Italy, Latvia and Slovakia, and 20 per cent in Romania' (Special Eurobarometer 449).

Non-consensual sex in the West

During my investigation in 2018, I discovered that in many countries in Europe, sex without consent is not rape.

There are twenty European countries which have ratified the Istanbul Convention (2011) but most of them have not changed their laws yet.

Only Belgium, Germany, Cyprus, UK, Luxemburg, Ireland,

Sweden and Iceland have enacted consent-based legislation. Germany did it in 2016 and in March 2018, Iceland did it.

In October 2012, three men raped a 15-year old girl in Sweden. They inserted a wine bottle into her private parts and made her bleed. The Swedish court acquitted the three accused men, ruling that the girl's refusal to open her legs indicated her 'shyness'. (They were later convicted in the court of appeal.)

Finally, in May 2018, Sweden passed a new law saying that sex without consent is rape.

The unique Indian scenario: criminalisation by parents

There is something unique that has happened in India which we don't see in the western nations and that is the criminalisation of consensual sex between partners which is done by their parents. It was revealed that one third of the rape cases that went to a full trial in Delhi district courts in 2013 were the cases in which young people had consensual sex without their parent's approval. When their parents found out they used the criminal justice system to end the relationship (Rukmini Shrinivasan).

It was also revealed that in 25 per cent of the total rape cases, women had filed cases against those men who had broken the promise to marry them (Rukmini Shrinivasan).

In India, if a man promises to marry a woman and then changes his mind, he can be charged with falsely obtaining consent for sex.

In 2017, Delhi High Court observed that 'number of cases where both persons, out of their own will and choice, develop a consensual physical relationship, when the relationship breaks due to some reason, the women use the law as a weapon for vengeance and personal vendetta'.

In 2019, India's supreme court said: There is a clear distinction between rape and consensual sex. The court, in such cases, must very carefully examine whether the accused had actually wanted to marry the victim or had mala fide motives and had made a false promise to this effect only to satisfy his lust, as the latter falls within the ambit of cheating or deception. There is also a distinction between mere breach of a promise and not fulfilling a false promise. If the accused has not made the promise with the sole intention of seducing the prosecutrix to indulge in sexual acts, such an act would not amount to rape.

In terms of creating a safe environment for women, India has a long way to go but one thing that becomes quickly very clear is that it needs to find its own solutions for its unique problems.

The findings from the recent Global Childhood Report 2019 were encouraging: 'India has greatly reduced child marriage through legal reforms, programmes to educate and empower girls, and public awareness campaigns...In South Asia, the most impressive gains have been in India, where child marriage is down 51 per cent since 2000 (from 30 to 15 per cent) and 63 per cent since 1990.'

Campus rape

In the USA, 80 per cent of college rapes and sexual assaults go unreported to police, as the Department of Justice, Office of Justice Programs, Bureau of Justice Statistics in the USA has pointed out. A study by the Association of American Universities (AAU) revealed chilling details of extent of sexual abuse in American colleges. As many as 23 per cent of American female college students have experienced some form of unwanted sexual contact. More than 600,000 international students (2017) study in Australia.

ABS (Australian Bureau of Statistics 2014-15) valued exports from international education at $18.8 billion, making it Australia's third largest export industry.

A recent report revealed that 51 per cent of students were sexually harassed in 2016. (Source: Australian Human Rights Commission).

Only nine per cent of students who experienced sexual assault on campus (in 2015 or 2016) reported it to their university.

The situation is also very frightening in the UK, where it was revealed that one-third of female students had experienced some form of sexual assault or abuse at university, says Youth Sight, in a study report commissioned by *The Telegraph*.

Even children and teens are not safe. In America, a 2011 survey found that 11.8 per cent of girls from grades 9-12 were forced to have sexual intercourse at some time in their lives (CDC).

In France, a study which was conducted in two major public universities reported that one in five women are victims of sexual assault in college, according to a Campus Sexual Assault study in 2007.

Pedophilia

According to the former Deputy Children's Commissioner for England (Sue Berelowitz), the number of pedophiles in the UK is so high that there is not enough land in the country to build the number of prisons required.

Chief Constable Simon Bailey (National Police Chiefs Council Lead for child protection) said that pedophiles who view indecent images (pornographic images/videos) of children should not be charged/jailed unless they pose a physical threat to children. According to him, the police forces are not able to cope with the huge number of cases.

A recent study which was financed by the European Union. closely analysed international child sexual abuse material (child pornography). The study revealed that 78.8 per cent of visible offenders were white.[7]

Online behaviour of pedophiles and the economic mechanism behind their activity were studied and the results were disturbing. It was revealed that most of the companies that handle servers which permit the functioning of many websites where child sexual abuse material (child pornography) is spread are actually located in Europe and America (Annual Report 2017, Pedophilia and Child Pornography, Associazione Meter).

The demand of child sex tourism is 'usually recognised as coming from the industrialised countries, including the richer countries of Europe, North America, the Russian Federation, Japan, Australia and New Zealand'.[8]

Pedophilia – a well-established British culture?

In the UK, in recent years, numerous reports have surfaced, which tend to point towards the Muslim immigrants for sexual crimes against children. However, questions need to be asked if such reports actually reveal the true British pedophile scenario.

Unfortunately, child abuse and pedophilia are nothing new in Great Britain.

Historically, many Britishers have advocated to legalising 'sex with children'.

7 Towards a Global Indicator on Unidentified Victims in Child Sexual Exploitation Material, Technical Report.

8 Report of the Special Rapporteur on the sale of children, child prostitution and child pornography, Najat MaallaM'jid, submitted to the Human Rights Council, UN, 2012.

Thomas Victor O'Carroll was a chair of the Pedophile Information Exchange (PIE). Headquartered in London, the group advocated for legal acceptance of pedophilia.

O'Carroll campaigned to lower the age of sexual consent to 10. In 2015, he joined the Labour Party of the UK.

Even the former British Prime Minister, Edward Heath, was accused of sexually abusing children. In 2014, 114 files connected to paedophile activity in Westminster strangely went 'missing'.

Jimmy Savile, who was an English media personality, was knighted in 1990. He hosted many shows on the BBC.

Steven Walker, who is a UNICEF Children's Champion, wrote in Morning Star Online, 'Some staff at the BBC have admitted they knew of his (Savile's) activities but declined to report him to the police as he was a big star drawing big audiences. He was a Tory supporter, friendly with Margaret Thatcher and duly rewarded with a knighthood in 1990, the same year Pope John Paul II awarded him a Papal Knighthood'.

Walker goes on further, stating:

'One of Tony Blair's former senior aides Phillip Lyon, who previously arranged his weekly prime minister's question time, was arrested after police raided his Commons office. Lyon was found guilty of downloading child pornography and jailed for a year. Stephen Carnell, who was an agent for Labour MP Chris Bryant during the 2010 general election campaign, was caught with more than 12,000 indecent images and 450 films. He was jailed for three years for collecting and distributing what the judge described as 'appalling' images of child sexual abuse'. (Source: Steven Walker, Morning Star Online, UK).

In July 2013, the university of Cambridge in the UK hosted academics in a conference who said paedophilia is 'normal and natural'.

What I have just mentioned here is just the tip of the iceberg.

Is it right to say that the UK has a well-established and continuous pedophile culture that is deeply rooted in its history and has even received political support?

If the Britishers could do it to their own people, one is also forced to think about what they must have done to people in the countries they colonised. If 114 files connected to pedophile activity in Westminster can strangely go 'missing' in 2014 in the UK, it is quite disturbing to even imagine what must have been done to hide the British sins in the countries they colonised.

This just does not only occur in the UK, across the western world, pedophile culture and the demands to make it legal have been observed on numerous occasions.

In Germany, the members of Europe's most influential environmentalist party – Germany's Greens' members supported paedohpile groups which demanded to legalise sex with children.

USA has its North American Man/Boy Love Association (NAMBLA) who advocated to legalise pedophlia and Switzerland has its Schweizerische Arbeitsgemeinschaft Pädophile.

The Australian Paedophile Support Group (APSG) in Australia, CRIES of Belgium, Fondation Nouvelle of Canada, the Danish Pedophile Association of Denmark, the GRED of France, Enclave Kring of Holland...the list of the pro-pedophilia groups in the western world is quite long.

Americans adopting foreign children to abuse them?

One of the worst possible examples of humans abusing other humans could be the abuse of differently-abled children or children who are orphans. An orphan who gets adopted hopes for a new home, a new start and lots of affection from the adopter.

However, that might not always be the case, if the adopter is a pedophile from a rich western nation.

In 2012, quite sensationally, the Russian President banned the adoption of Russian children by American citizens.

On many occasions, children who are adopted from foreign nations are listed like commodities in America and all this takes place quite openly.

Americans are big at adopting foreign children. They have adopted nearly 243,000 children from other countries since the late 1990s (Reuters, 2013).

For most developing countries like India, when a potential adopter from a developed country like the USA shows interest in adopting an orphan, the local authorities tend to feel grateful. But no one knows exactly what is in store for the orphan child once he or she is sent away.

In 2013, an investigation revealed chilling details of how foreign children who were once adopted from abroad were being listed online in the USA. Children who were adopted from countries like Russia, China, Ukraine, Ethiopia (aged 6-14) were listed. The investigation analysed 5,029 such posts from a five-year period. The youngest child was just 10 months old (Reuters, 2013).

Here is an example of such an advertisement:

Born in October of 2000 – this handsome boy, 'Rick' was placed from India a year ago and is obedient and eager to please (Reuters, 2013).

On various occasions, children are victims of severe abuse.

'...a Russian girl, recounted how a boy in one house urinated on her after the two had sex; she was 13 at the time and was re-homed three times in six months.' (Reuters, 2013).

No authority tracks what happens after a child is brought to America, so no one knows how often international adoptions fail. The US government estimates that domestic adoptions fail at a rate ranging from 'about 10 to 25 per cent'. If international adoptions fail with the same frequency, then more than 24,000 foreign adoptees are no longer with the parents who brought them to the United States. (Reuters, 2013.)

Are Indian authorities and Indian media even aware of this situation?

Sexual abuse in foster care and child sex offences

In the US, about one in 10 children are sexually abused (Darkness to Light, USA).

The Centers for Disease Control and Prevention revealed that in the USA, among all female victims of completed rape, 41 per cent were raped prior to age 18, and 30 per cent were raped between the age of 11 and 17.

American children who live in the child welfare system face a higher risk of experiencing sexual abuse and exploitation. (Source: Sexual Abuse of State Wards, Youth in Adoptive or Guardian Homes, & Youth In Residential Placement, reported July 2013-October 2016).

The country's foster care system is also a source of sex-trafficked kids (NCMEC, USA).

Even children rape other children.

In October 2017, it was revealed that since 2013, police had received nearly 30,000 reports of children committing sexual offences in England and Wales (38 of the 43 police forces).

This included rapes that took place on school premises and on primary school playgrounds.[9]

A Freedom of Information request submitted by *Sun Online* showed that children as young as five were suspected of committing rape in London (between 2012 and 2017).

According to NSPCC (UK), a third of all child sexual offences are committed by children and young people.

In the UK, more than 64,000 child sex offences were reported to police within a 12-month period (in 2016/2017).

Crimes included rape, grooming and sexual assault.

More than 13,800 were against children aged 10 or under.

Nearly 200 were against babies under the age of one. (Figures obtained by NSPCC through FOI.)

Bestiality

It is well-known that meat consumption rate is very high in the western nations (as shown in Picture 4).

Animals are not only slaughtered for their meat but also, they are sexually abused.

For years, erotic zoos and animal brothels were openly thriving in Germany. Finally, the government in Germany passed a law in 2013 which aimed to stop the abuse. Since then, there have been demands to legalise bestiality.[10]

In Denmark, a 2011 Justice Ministry report found that 17 per cent of veterinarians suspected that a human had had sex with an animal that they treated.

9 Figures obtained through Freedom of Information (FOI) by BBC's Panorama.
10 https://www.thelocal.de/20160218/top-court-throws-out-bid-to-legalize-bestiality

> William M. Fleming,[1] Brian Jory, and David L. Burton
>
> **Characteristics of Juvenile Offenders Admitting to Sexual Activity with Nonhuman Animals**
>
> ABSTRACT
>
> This study compared the family characteristics, victimization histories, and number of perpetration offenses of juvenile offenders who admitted to having had sex with animals to juvenile offenders who did not. The study found that 96% of the juveniles who had engaged in sex with nonhuman animals also admitted to sex offenses against humans and reported more offenses against humans than other sex offenders their same age and race. Those juveniles who had engaged in sex with animals were similar to

In 2015, Denmark banned bestiality as the country was aiming to stop its flourishing animals sex tourism, but bestiality still remained legal in Finland, Hungary, Romania and in several states of the USA.[11]

Can such bans change the habits of the people overnight? Is there a way these poor animals can report the tortures they go through?

Is there a connection between those who abuse animals and those who abuse humans?

A study found that 96 per cent of the juveniles who had engaged in sex with nonhuman animals also admitted to sex offenses against humans and reported more offenses against humans than other sex offenders their same age and race.

In 2017, a man was jailed in the UK for encouraging his 64-year old wife to have sex with three dogs. The act took place in

11 https://www.news.com.au/travel/travel-updates/denmark-bans-bestiality-in-bid-to-kerb-rise-in-animal-sex-tourism/news-story/9b0f28e8cbbaac0508bf66736d7a5b75

an animal sex party – a culture that thrives through back door channels in the UK.[12]

In the UK, an investigation revealed that online 'forums where zoo parties – human and animal orgies – are discussed are full of threads with advice for those arranging events for the first time. One woman describes how her first time was in front of her husband and eight other members of their BDSM group' (Metro.co.uk).

The culture of animal sex parties and animal sexual abuse is an unfortunate reality. A website https://thecrueltylistuk.com, lists many such episodes that frequently occur in Great Britain.

In 2016 in Australia, a Brisbane woman who had sex with her dog was set free from prison (*Daily Mail*).

To a great extent, these incidents do explain the culture of Bestialilty in the western nations. Perhaps, that is why in Germany, there has been a consistent demand to legalise bestiality ever since the government passed a law in 2013 which aimed to stop the animal abuse.

The Church

Church sexual abuse is a global story. The United Nations said that the Vatican should 'Immediately remove all known and suspected child sexual abusers from service and refer the matter to the relevant law enforcement authorities for investigation and prosecution'. (Source: United Nations, Convention on the Rights of the Child, 2014).

But, for the Vatican, Canon Law (Church law) is more important than the local criminal law.

---

12 https://www.mirror.co.uk/news/uk-news/husband-jailed-after-encouraging-64-10427993

A Church commissioned report which was criticised for undercounting revealed that more than 10,000 children were allegedly victimised. The report found that 4 per cent of all priests who had served in the USA from 1950 to 2002 had faced allegations of child sexual abuse (the John Jay report).

In Australia, 7 per cent of priests were accused of abusing children. As many as 40 per cent of St John of God Brothers were accused of abuse, sys the Royal Commission into Institutional Responses to Child Sexual Abuse. It is important to point out that many victims do not come forward because of fear or shame.

In Germany, the 2018 German Bishops' Conference published a report revealing that between 1946 and 2014, roughly 4.4 per cent of clerics were sexual abusers.

Controversially, in 2019, in the Holy Spirit Church of Münster, a retired priest dedicated his sermon encouraging the attendees to forgive priests who had sexually abused minors. *Deutsche Welle* reported that 'victims of abuse were said to have been present as the priest spoke'.[13]

In Feb 2019, for the first time Pope Francis publicly admitted that priests and bishops sexually abused nuns.

In Spain, a chilling incident of trafficking surfaced when it was revealed that 300,000 babies were stolen from their parents between 1939 and the 1990s (SOS Stolen Babies Association).

Child marriage

In the West, marriage is slowly becoming outdated but there is a particular section in America for whom marriages are very much in fashion.

---

13 Deutsche Welle, https://www.dw.com/en/german-priest-causes-church-walkout-as-preaches-for-predator-priest-forgiveness/a-49479695

But these are not normal marriages. These are marriages with children.

More than 240,000 children were married in the US between 2000 and 2010; 77 per cent of the children wed were minor girls married to adult men. (Source: Unchained At Last).

It is 2018 and in many states of the USA, children can get married at any age if certain conditions are met.

In Alaska, South Carolina and Louisiana, marriage licenses were granted to even 12-year old children.

Even a 74-year old man married a 14-year old girl.

Teachers abusing children in the USA

Multiple studies have shown that children who are forced to marry are less likely to have a proper education.

So, does that mean that all children who are studying in American schools are doing great?

A study revealed that more than 4.5 million public school children in the USA are subject to sexual misconduct by an employee of a school sometime between kindergarten and 12th grade.

It was found that 9.6 per cent of public school children in the USA face sexual misconduct from being told sexual jokes to sexual intercourse by educators.

It is absolutely frightening that even principals and teachers are involved in the sexual abuse of children. (Source: Shakeshaft, 2003; AAUW, 2001).

Children/students abusing teachers

In the UK, a survey by the NASUWT uncovered that one in five teachers were sexually harassed at school by pupil, parent, manager or a colleague since becoming a teacher.

About 81 per cent had suffered sexual harassment or bullying in the workplace. Thirty per cent of those who were sexually harassed were subjected to unwanted touching.

As many as 21 per cent were sexually propositioned and quite disturbingly three per cent had their photos taken (down blousing or up skirting).

Many changed their jobs, had a bad impact in their career progression and suffered from mental health issues. Many were forced to change their daily routine to avoid the harasser and many had to change their style of clothing.

As many as 42 per cent of victims (teachers) never reported incidents of sexual harassment citing reasons like that they would not be believed, or nothing would be done about it or feeling embarrassed or fearful.

Those who did complain did not always have a favorable result. Of those who reported the sexual harassment, in 21 per cent of incidents, no action was taken against the offender.

Sexual violence and sexual harassment between children is also a matter of great concern.

In the UK, a 2017 survey revealed that '64 per cent of girls aged 13-21 had experienced sexual violence or sexual harassment at school or college in the past year. This included 39 per cent having their bra strap pulled by a boy and 27 per cent having their skirts pulled up within the last week'.[14]

In the Military

The situation is equally terrible in the US military.

---

14 Sexual violence and sexual harassment between children in schools and colleges, Department for Education, UK.

An AP investigation found that in America, the single largest category of inmates in military prisons are child sex offenders.

In the US military, sexual violence mostly goes unreported. In the fiscal year ending September 2014, 18,900 military members experienced unwanted sexual contact. 4.3 per cent of active duty women faced it. Only 43 per cent of females reported.[15]

Athletes/sports-related

Sporting dreams of innocent children and sports talents are regularly crushed whether it is America's Gymnastics sex abuse scandal or Britain's football sexual abuse scandal.

Even the female gymnasts of the 2012 gold-medal winning US national team had to go through this.

In the UK, more than 260 politicians and celebrities were investigated for alleged child sex abuse. This included musicians, film stars and TV stars (T Whitehead, 2015).

Sexual harassment of high-ranked western women

In Europe, it has been found that even women who hold high ranks in their professional career are not safe when it comes to sexual abuse.

Joanna Goodey, the lead researcher on the Violence Against Women survey stated:

What did surprise me a bit was the fact that 75 per cent of women in top management and professional positions said that they have been victims of sexual harassment. And that's extremely high – even in the past 12 months the figures were pretty high for women in those positions (FRA).

15 Department of Defense, Fiscal Year 2014 Annual Report on Sexual Assault in the Military, (2015).

Pornography

Pornography is not only corelated to sex trafficking, drugs, crime and health issues, it has a major role in how our generation perceives sex. While porn is being promoted as a part of a healthy life-style among an ill-informed and vulnerable population of the developing countries, the experts and researchers of the developed countries are finding ways how to discourage people from watching porn. Reward Foundation is one such organisation. http://www.rewardfoundation.org/

At times, we Europeans wonder who will finally highlight our painful stories at the global forums? Is there somebody who will be able to cut through our glossy image that has been built by our soft power and highlight the well-established pattern of sexual abuse against our women and children?

Millions of women and children of Europe and America need to be heard too. Their tears are also important.

For instance, how many of us have heard of 'new wolf pack' gang of Spain, 'tournantes' (organised gang-rapes) of France and Operation Hydrant of the UK?

Did you know that a Spanish company – ExoClick – whose advertisements have been hosted by a revenge porn website (responsible for promoting rape culture and destroying many lives) was recognised as one of the fastest-growing private companies in Europe by Inc. 5000 Europe and it had even won The Business of the Year award in 2016 from the European Business Awards?

When things surfaced, the company innocently claimed that they were not aware of the situation. The revenge porn site – Anon-IB – ruined the lives of many innocent girls, many of whom were underage. It was eventually shutdown by the Dutch police but as expected, the users later migrated to other platforms.

Millions of women in Europe were raped during the World War.

Even without a war, millions of our (European) women and children have been raped.

Decades have passed but Indigenous women are still facing violence in Canada, Australia and America. They are being raped and they are still going missing.[16]

Why is it happening? Where did things go so wrong? Have these societies become overly sexualised?

Why is the media in Europe or in America not speaking loud enough? Why are we not ready to admit our own wrongdoings? In Europe, the media has kept our people ill-informed. Why? Should we call it willful deceit? Or is it white elitism?

India wants to protect its women. But how will India do it? Will it blindly import the failed foreign experiments, or will it create its own unique model for its unique situation?

The world does not need lessons on women's safety from Europeans and we do not even deserve to be the role models. Instead, we need help to protect our own people.

This is an epidemic and we are still in denial. Deceitful use of our media's soft power will not hide our crimes forever.

They are emotionally corrupted minds and there are emotionally corrupted societies.

No amount of suppression or repression of sexual desire will work. Unless psychologically damaged minds are healed, societies cannot be healed.

16 Source: Missing and Murdered Aboriginal Women: A National Operational Overview, Canada.

NINE

WHAT CAUSES BROKEN FAMILIES IN THE WEST?

'Vicious cycles': can we turn the clock?

GLOBALLY, DEVELOPED nations have the highest rates of alcohol use.

Alcohol is a big part of the mainstream western culture even though it is well-documented that alcohol, child abuse, domestic violence, Fetal Alcohol Spectrum Disorders (FASD), crimes are corelated and hurt economy and health in multiple ways.

But why is alcohol such a big part of the western societies?

'There are four main reasons why people drink: to be social, to create a positive mood, to cope, or to conform.' Dinking patterns differ across the world, shaped by the local context of where people live, including local laws, regulations, and policies related to alcohol; history, cultural and religious beliefs and attitudes; and, the social determinants of health. In addition, major political, economic and social events can influence a country's drinking pattern.

Numerous studies have scientifically connected alcohol to various serious issues which are very well – explained in the graph below:

A SCCHEMATTIC OF THE WIDESPREAD IMPACTS OF ALCOHOL ON RISKY BEHAVIOUR

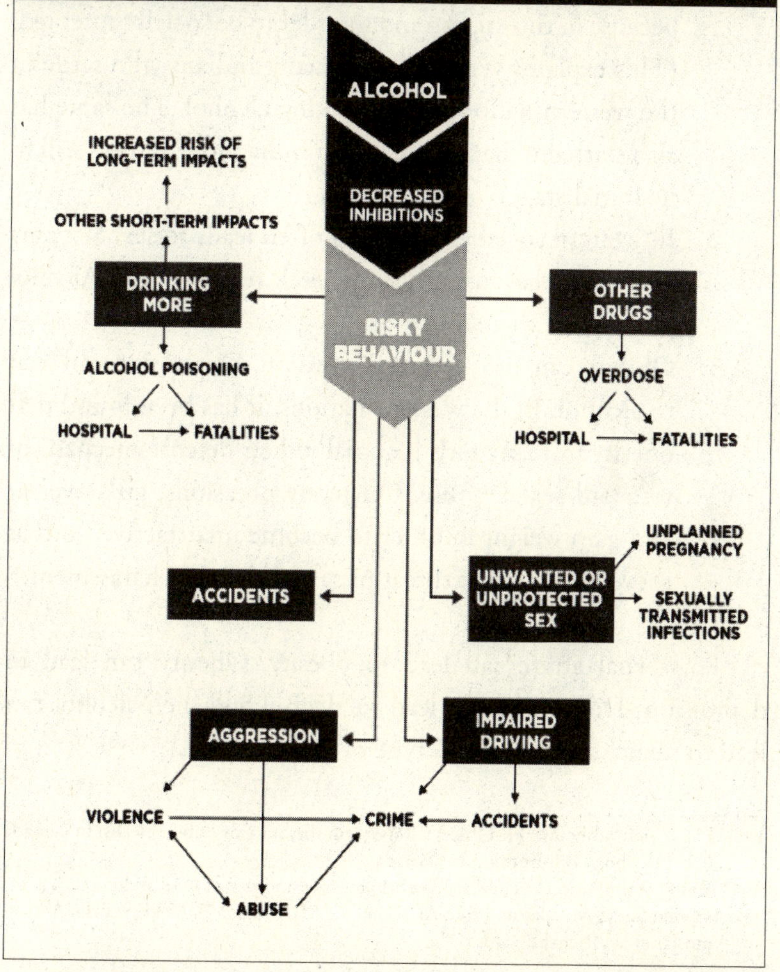

A closer look at the chart above certainly shows some sort of multiple vicious cycles that western societies have found themselves stuck in. A few points that must be noted:

1. When a drug is socially acceptable, people are more likely to use it and pressure others to use it too. Non-drinkers can be reluctant to disclose their non-drinking status because of this stigma and in order to be socially accepted. (This explains very well why many Indians who settle in the western nations start drinking alcohol. The same has also started to happen in urban India, however it is still in its initial stage)[1]
2. In western societies, drinking often leads to sex. Sex may lead to a relationship. People seek relationships. Alcohol plays a role there too.
3. Obesity can also lead to depression. Depression can lead to alcohol. In the western nations, it has been found that obesity in many girls is actually their defense mechanism to avoid sexual abuse. On many occasions, girls overeat and gain weight in order to become unattractive, so that they can avoid the threat of sexual abuse or harassment.[2]

So, sexual abuse can lead to obesity. Obesity can lead to depression. Depression can lead to alcohol and then alcohol can lead to sexual abuse again. A type of vicious cycle.

---

1 The Chief Public Health Officer's Report on the State of Public,Health in Canada 2015,Alcohol Consumption In Canada

2 Abuse victimisation in childhood or adolescence and risk of food addiction in adult women Susan M. Mason, PhD, Alan J. Flint, MD, Alison E. Field, S. Bryn Austin, and Janet W. Rich-Edwards

Another study confirms the connection between sexual abuse and obesity in the West:

'Among the various psychosocial etiologies contributing to obesity, childhood sexual abuse and trauma is an important factor. As much as 16 per cent of adult men and 25 per cent of adult women in the general population report a history of some form of childhood sexual abuse. Childhood sexual abuse survivours have been found significantly more likely to become obese (42 per cent) in young adulthood than non-abused individuals (28 per cent). Interestingly, the obesity in this patient population has been shown to be relatively treatment resistant.'[3]

4. The situation becomes pretty irreversible when 'mind-altering drugs' become socially acceptable, as it has happened in the West. The normalisation of such behaviour has reached such an extent that even parents, guardians and other family members have become the source for the alcohol for underage drinkers. The alcohol culture in western homes can be held responsible. An American survey revealed that 'Fifty-four per cent of current underage drinkers reported family and friends as their source for the alcohol they consumed – parents/guardians/other adult family member (27 per cent), another underage person (17 per cent), took from home (7 per cent), took from someone else's home (3 per cent)' (Key Substance Use and Mental Health Indicators in the United States: Results from the 2017 National Survey on Drug Use and Health).

3 Obesity as a defense mechanism Justin Fadena, Douglas Leonarda, John O'Reardona, Robin Hansonb.

In 2012, it was found that more than 10 per cent of American children live with a parent who has alcohol problems (Substance Abuse and Mental Health Services Administration, SAMHSA).

Underage drinking has serious consequences and is responsible for risky behavior. (Check Flowchart above) In addition, it has also been found that 40 per cent of those who initiate drinking under the age of 15 end up getting diagnosed as 'alcohol dependent' at some point in their lives.[4]

Above points clearly indicate that in the western nations, an alcohol based vicious cycle has formed. In other words, alcohol leads to alcohol again (after causing multiple damages including sex crimes).

A typical traditional Indian family is generally very critical of alcohol. From a rational point of view, it makes a lot of sense. No, it is not moral policing, it is actually a scientific consultation which can empower our youngsters so that they are well-informed before they make their 'own independent decisions'.

Even in America, the Indian community is in the group with the lowest usage of illicit drugs and alcohol (National Survey On Drug Use And Health). As western commercial monoculture is taking over India gradually, with pubs and discotheques popping up like mushrooms, one must ask where India might end up if it continues getting Americanised blindly.

Unmarried mothers, single parents and broken families

A strong family bond is still very important for an average Indian. Generally, Indians are critical of divorces and the divorcees.

---

4 Grant BF, and Dawson, DA. Age at onset of alcohol use and its association with DSM-IV alcohol abuse and dependence: Results from the National Longitudinal Alcohol Epidemiologic Survey. J Sub Abuse 9:103-110, 1997.

Alcohol usage is also related to divorces and separation of partner.

It was found that women's drinking is most common between ages 26 and 34 and among women who are either separated or divorced.[5]

'Negative family relationships, including divorce and family violence, are associated with more or earlier drinking' and on the other hand 'Positive family relationships and parenting practices are linked to reduced drinking by teenagers'.[6]

Without an element of doubt, marriages which suffer from partner abuse should end in divorce or separation. But does it mean that single parenting and nonmarital childbearing should be encouraged and glorified? Numerous studies have indicated that high divorce rates, single parenting and broken families… such scenarios are only making things worse in the western world, whether it is family financial crisis, alcohol abuse / drug abuse or sexual abuse.

In developing nations like India which are increasingly getting influenced by the western commercial monoculture, the thought of staying single and unmarried is at times considered bold, progressive and empowering. But are such people really well-informed?

In America, a 2011 study revealed that the riskiest home situation for children was living with one parent and an unmarried partner as 57.2 per 1,000 children were maltreated.

---

5 Su SS, Larison C, Ghadialy R et al. Substance Use Among Women in the United States. SAMHSA Analytic Series A-3. Rockville, MD: Substance Abuse and Mental Health Services Administration, 1997.

6 The Chief Public Health Officer's Report on the State of Public Health in Canada 2015, Alcohol Consumption In Canada.

The risk was more than eight times higher than what it would be with both biological parents and more than twice higher than what it would be in a single-parent household (2011 federal study).

It was also revealed that children who live with a single parent that has a live-in partner are at the highest risk of sexual abuse. In comparison to the children who live with their biological parents, they are 20 times more likely to be victims of sexual abuse (Fourth National Incidence Study of Child Abuse and Neglect, NIS-4 Report to Congress).

According to Alan Davis, head of the National Council on Child Abuse and Family Violence, 'incest is more likely to occur in a family where at least one parent is a stepparent and it shows up far more often in homes where both parents are not the natural parents'.[7]

In terms of finishing college, graduating from high school and becoming gainfully employed, children who grow up in married, intact families perform far better than their peers who grow up in nonintact families. Not only that, they are also more likely to enjoy a stable family life themselves.[8]

Adolescents who do not belong to an intact married family are more likely to get suspended or expelled from school, get involved in a fight, be involved in crimes like theft and get arrested (National Longitudinal Study of Adolescent Health. Adolescents Grades 7-12 & National longitudinal survey of youth).

On the other hand, children who live with their biological

---

7 http://www.nydailynews.com/life-style/health/warning-signs-incest-learn-mackenzie-phillips-article-1.403354.

8 Ron Haskins and Isabel Sawhill, Creating an Opportunity Society (Washington, DC: The Brookings Institution, 2009); Nicholas H Wolfinger, Understanding the Divorce Cycle: The Children of Divorce in Their Own Marriages (New York: Cambridge University Press, 2005).

parents are among the least contacted by schools over behavioural problems, says the National survey of children's health 2003.

Well, with a far stronger family bond than their counterparts, to an extent this does explain one of the reasons why the Indian community is so successful in the USA.

The links between happy marriages and healthy brains have been confirmed as well.

In the UK, researchers at University College London explored the link between marital status and dementia and found that those who lead their whole life as single are 42 per cent more likely than married people to suffer from dementia in later life.[9]

Researches have shown that happily married people live an overall better life than those who remain single. 'For example, as compared with those who are single, those who are married tend to live longer, have fewer strokes and heart attacks, have a lower chance of becoming depressed, be less likely to have advanced cancer at the time of diagnosis and more likely to survive cancer for a longer period of time', says Robert H Shmerling, MD, Faculty Editor, Harvard Health Publishing.

The culture of having multiple sex-partners has not benefitted either.

It has been found that Americans who have 'only ever slept with their spouses' are most likely to report being in a 'very happy' marriage, reports sociologist Nicholas Wolfinger, of the University of Utah.

A Princeton University and Harvard University study has

9 Marriage and risk of dementia: systematic review and meta-analysis of observational studies, Andrew Sommerlad, Joshua Ruegger, Archana Singh-Manoux, Glyn Lewis, Gill Livingston.

found that more than half of 'all American children will likely live with an unmarried mother at some point before they reach age 18'.

In the UK (England and Wales), nearly half of all children are born to unmarried mothers, says the Office for National Statistics, UK, 2013.

It is well documented that single parents face a disproportionate risk of poverty. In the UK, it was found that single parents have the highest poverty rate among working age households. In 2017, there were nearly 1.7 million single-parent families in the UK.[10]

Similar results have also been found elsewhere. In Sweden, a report revealed that single-parent homes children suffer from more psychosomatic problems.[11]

In America, studies have revealed that children who are born to unmarried mothers not only suffer from socio-emotional problems but also have a higher chance of experiencing unstable living arrangements and poverty.

After reaching adolescence, they are more likely to engage in sex at a younger age and have a birth outside of marriage. Poorer educational attainment, lower occupational status, lower income, more divorces and troubled marriages are the other problems that they face as young adults (Births to Unmarried Women - Child Trends).

Again, a vicious cycle (unmarried mothers giving birth to children who may later themselves become unmarried mothers) has formed in such a situation, apart from other 'vicious cycles' that I have already discussed in this chapter.

---

10 One in four – A profile of single parents in the UK, Gingerbread, 2018.

11 Fifty moves a year:Is there an association between joint physical custody and psychosomatic problems in children? MalinBergström, Emma Fransson, BitteModin, Marie Berlin, Per A Gustafsson, Anders Hjern.

The absence of a known biological father can also increase the chances of a child showing behaviours like aggression, delinquency and rule breaking (*What happens to children of unmarried mothers,* By Sara McLanahan and Christopher Jencks).

The absence of a father is also linked to early sexual activity and teenage pregnancy in daughters and an elevated risk of youth incarceration in males.[12]

Conversely, a close parent-adolescent bond is linked with the increased use of contraceptives and birth control to delay sexual activity and decrease in the likelihood of teen pregnancy. (Source: Boonstra, HD (2011) Teen pregnancy among young women in foster care: a primer. *Guttmacher Policy Review*).

Again, the above indicators do explain to an extent why the Indian system of family structure has delivered brilliant results in America.

For example, Indians lead every other ethnic group in the US socioeconomically. In terms of family structure, Indian Americans are 'more likely to be currently married than US adults overall and to have lower rates of birth outside of marriage' (Pew Research Center).

Broken family leading to 'lost custody of children'

The western nations scenario

Foster care population has everything to do with broken families, divorces, higher sexual abuse and single motherhood. 'Federal data reveals that between 50 and 80 per cent of children in foster care

12 Does Father Absence Place Daughters at Special Risk for Early Sexual Activity and Teenage Pregnancy? Bruce J Ellis, John E Bates, Kenneth A Dodge, David M Fergusson, L John Horwood, Gregory S Pettit, andLianne Woodward.
Father Absence and Youth Incarceration Cynthia C Harper University of California San Francisco Sara S McLanahan Princeton University.

have been removed from households headed by single mothers or unmarried couples' and ironically, children who enter a foster care system often grow up to be teen/adults who give birth to children that end up in welfare system again. It has been documented that teen mothers in foster care are far more likely to lose custody of babies.[13]

So, again the 'vicious cycle' centered around the foster care system just continues.

In the USA,

a) Foster children are 10 times more likely to be sexually abused than children who live with their both biological parents, according to the Fourth National Incidence Study of Child Abuse and Neglect (NIS–4) Report to Congress.
b) One half (49 per cent) of females who were ever in foster care during their youth experienced forced sex (either before, during, or after their time in foster care), a per centage that is more than four times that for females nationwide (11 per cent), says 2011 Teen Parents study.
c) By the age of 19, girls who had been in foster care were two and a half times more likely than the girls nationwide to have become pregnant (48 versus 20 per cent) and nearly three times more likely to have had a child (32 versus 12 per cent), the same study explains.
d) Approximately 65 per cent of girls and 40 per cent of boys who had ever been in foster care had sexual intercourse before the age of 16, compared with 35 per cent of girls

13 Teen Parents in Foster Care: Risk Factors and Outcomes for Teens and Their Children By Jennifer Manlove, PhD, Kate Welti, MPP, Marci McCoyRoth, MA, Amanda Berger, PhD, and Karin Malm, MS 2011.
Elizabeth Wall-Wieler, 2018, Canada.

and 33 per cent of boys who had never been in foster care, the study adds.

e) Various types of crimes have a connection with foster care upbringing: 'Teens in foster care were at least twice as likely as were teens living at home to report substance use; four times as likely to have carried a gun to school; and twice as likely to have been in a physical fight at school or to be a gang member', the *Teen Parents* study adds.

The Foster care system is also a source of sex-trafficked kids (NCMEC, USA).

The kids in the foster care system are also victims who on many occasions become perpetrators as they grow up. American children who live in the child welfare system face a higher risk of experiencing sexual abuse and exploitation.

So, as India becomes more and more Americanised, its families will get broken, divorces rate will get higher, its population in foster care (or a similar welfare system) will increase and will give birth to such multiple vicious cycles that the USA is facing, something that is not very easy to reverse.

And let us not forget, establishing and maintaining a welfare system can be a big burden to a nation's economy too. '…teen childbearing costs US taxpayers billions of dollars through welfare payments and other assistance and through social services, such as health care and child welfare', the Teen Parents study found.

Understanding the FASD angle

When a 29-year old American woman – Brandi Holmes was convicted of murder on New Year's Day 2003 of Julian Brandon, FAS was being discussed.

Due to the mother's alcohol use, nearly 20-50 children per 1,000 are born with FASD in the USA.[14]

The offender's attorneys argued that she acted like a 10-12-year old. It was due to FAS. The syndrome causes brain damage, sexual behavioural problems and intellectual disabilities.

While the systematic promotion of alcohol as something 'cool' and 'empowering' continues to take place among the females of the developing countries, the relation of FAS and sexual crimes is increasingly being examined in the West, where many governments are running campaigns to encourage women to give up alcohol, so that fetus does not suffer from FAS.

In other words, women who drink alcohol during pregnancy, are more likely to give birth to children who are more likely to commit FAS-induced sex crimes when they grow up. In the greater scheme of things, how can anyone consider this behaviour to be empowering for women, which is directly connected to the increase in number of sex crimes?

So, is the situation already beyond repair? Can India empower its women by blindly following the failed western model? When things eventually get worse, will India regret and try to simply turn the clock back to recreate the strong family bond of its bygone era or will it be proactive enough to empower its citizens by spreading awareness that can help its citizens make independent and wiser decisions before the situation becomes completely irreversible?

---

14 Source: May, Prevalence and epidemiologic characteristics of FASD from various research methods with an emphasis on recent in-school studies. Developmental Disabilities Research Reviews.
Prevalence and characteristics of fetal alcohol spectrum disorders. May PA.

Are these minds 'psychologically damaged'?

Sexual relationships with stepchildren are also an American reality. At times, mothers and daughters compete for the same boyfriend.

Cases like having sex with the stepchild and then murdering the husband (the Susan Grund incident) or incidents of daughter and mother competing for the same man, many complex situations have been surfacing in the western societies after their experiment with sexual liberty (the Julie Andrews incident or Woody Allan incident).

After the infamous 'Nirbhaya' incident in New Delhi, the Indian administration did feel the pressure to take the necessary steps to improve the situation but did the Australian government do enough when an Australian couple was found kidnapping children and raping them? (The Sian Kingi incident.)

Did the USA do enough after a pedophile was arrested who even wanted to kill the American president and even had a radioactive material? (The Cummings incident.)

American husband and wife gangs who kidnap girls in their moving car and rape them may create some fear in their immediate neighbourhood but unfortunately, such incidents do not always inspire foreign governments to issue a travel advisory for tourists who visit America and do not create enough global attention. (The Rosemary West incident, Alvin and Judith Neelley incident, Buttrum Janice incident.)

When a Chinese student was brutally raped and murdered in Germany, safety alerts or safety advisories were not issued in India, especially when Germany is such a popular destination for many Indian students. Why?

Why were Indian students not issued regular travel advisories regarding the British 'happy slapping' culture?

Why did the reputation of the Silicon Valley in America not take a hit when a couple (man and woman) abducted a 22-year old girl from the street, kept her inside their car, tied her with hooks and ropes, tortured her, gaged and strangled her and eventually killed her, all of that not too far away from Silicon Valley (Source: Michaud Michelle incident). Why protests were not held in Silicon Valley like they were held by Indians in New Delhi after the 'Nirbhaya' incident?

Why can we Europeans and our brothers and sisters in America not learn how to speak loud against violent crimes as much as Indians do? Why does the western media not highlight these issues at global forums?

Are western societies sexualised beyond repair?

Well, in the UK, one can legally have a naked girl coming to clean one's house. For many it may sound very disgusting and sick but of course, it is real, and it is happening. These girls who provide naked cleaning services in their client homes are paid around 50 pounds an hour and there are many agencies who are providing such services. One can avail such services by just a simple google search.

In order to understand the mentality of some of these western country citizens, one should take note of many frequent cases of virginity auctions, a trend in the western countries in which young teenage girls sell their virginity online to the highest bidder. From virginity auctions and naked maids to western women visiting foreign countries for sex tourism, where even underage boys are also hired are some of the disturbing stories which are not completely unheard of.

For many western women, sex with underage boys may be possible without having to go to Africa for it.

A Swedish study revealed that nearly six per cent of the adult female participants had engaged in some sort of sex with underage males and 2.4 per cent had had sexual intercourse with underage males.[15]

How many of us know about the 'free sex commune' culture of the West? How many of us have heard of 'Rockbitch'?

Have we shown enough concern regarding the scale of abuse that has been reported in 'The Children of God' cult in the West? The cult is known to encourage sex with children. It is also known for pressurising women to convert others by soliciting sex.

Through their practice 'flirty fishing', which according to their founder was based on a quote from the Bible, the women in the group are supposed to go ''fishing' for new members.

Imagine the life of those children who are born in such western cults. Have we shown enough concern regarding them? Has the western media done enough to highlight these issues globally? The group is now known as 'The Family International'.

On its website, it explains itself as 'an online Christian network of individuals in nearly 80 countries, committed to sharing the message of God's love with others'.

Such incidents may not sound very shocking in such western societies where politicians advertise for their election campaign on porn websites (e.g. Denmark politician advertising on an adult website) and government backed groups openly advocate for incest by claiming that relationship between sisters and brothers should be seen as 'a fundamental right'.[16]

15 Exhibitionism and Sex with Underage Males in Adult Women, Sandra S Stroebel, Stephen L O'Keefe, Karen Griffee, Karen Harper-Dorton.

16 Incest a 'fundamental right', German committee:https://www.telegraph.co.uk/news/worldnews/europe/germany/11119062/Incest-a-fundamental-right-German-committee-says.html.

How many of us know that in the USA, 20 million Americans have been victims of parental incest as children? (Doak, Melissa J Child Abuse and Domestic Violence. New York, NY: Gale Cengage Learning, 2011.)

Yes, incest is a reality. In Finland, 0.5 per cent incidence of FDI was found in a random sample consisting of 3,757 female Finnish ninth grade students (Sariola and Uutela, 1996).

In the UK, a mother and her son came out saying that they enjoy 'mind-blowing sex' together.[17]

Incidents like a boy meeting his girlfriend's father only to realise that he had also once slept with the father are not completely unheard of. Can this be also called 'incest'?[18]

In France, there is a nudist town Cap d'Agde where nudists walk free in the whole town doing their daily activities. It is a very famous tourist destination and attracts visitors from all over Europe.

According to the XIV Congress of the International Naturist Federation (Agde, France, 1974) naturism is defined as follows:'a way of life in harmony with nature characterised by the practice of communal nudity with the intention of encouraging self-respect, respect for others and for the environment.'

But the question that I would like to raise is that is there a way to find out that an individual who is claiming to be a naturist is actually not an exhibitionist?

---

17 https://www.dailymail.co.uk/news/article-3531232/British-mother-son-enjoy-mind-blowing-sex-hiding-police-say-face-15-years-jail.html.

18 https://www.theguardian.com/lifeandstyle/2019/mar/12/i-met-my-girlfriends-parents-and-realised-i-had-once-slept-with-her-father?fbclid=IwAR0gedVYWrqyat89wbSUWJK4WsiwnETIguGYQQlBadLenBbDx0qloPySfpo.

Exhibitionism or indecent exposure have been classified as a sexual offence; as per law in many countries, it is considered a 'mental disorder' (Charles Lasègue) and it has been confirmed that exhibitionists feel sexual arousal during their act of exposures of genitals.[19]

Can someone explain how such behaviour can be considered respectful? Can the International Naturist Federation confirm that all visitors who visit the nude French town are not exhibitionists?

As far as the respect for the environment is concerned, can we please have the calculations of the 'ecological footprint' of an average visitor of Cap d Agde and see where it stands in the Global footprint network's metrics?

Strong urges for indecent exposure in public does exist in western societies. A Swedish study found that more than 10 per cent of participants had exposed themselves in public and more than 5 per cent had strong urges to do so.

It was also found that 'exposure to nudity within the nuclear family and partnered early sexual experimentation involving breast or genital exposure' significantly increases the likelihood of urges that lead to 'public exposure'.[20]

So, is the western urge to get nude or wear revealing clothes a sign of women empowerment/a progressive act/modern behavior or just an undiagnosed/hidden exhibitionism?

In a recent development, when one of the biggest YouTube Channels in the world openly mocked and shamed Indians after cherry-picking a few examples of sexually explicit online messages

---

19 Nolen-Hoeksema, Susan (2014). Abnormal Psychology (6th ed.).

20 Exhibitionism and Sex with Underage Males in Adult Women, Sandra S Stroebel, Stephen L O'Keefe, Karen Griffee, Karen Harper-Dorton.

(which were written in wrongly spelled English) that some Indian men had sent to western women, the perception of an average Indian man on YouTube almost changed forever. The YouTuber shouldn't be taken lightly because he alone generates more views than many well-established news outlets. He alone is capable of changing perceptions of millions of people overnight.

New insulting 'tags' like b*** and V***** were just added in the vocabulary to insult and stereotype Indians. Note: no comparative statistics exists for Indian women being propositioned by aged, white males. As a concerned global citizen, one should condemn online harassment through messages regardless of the offender's nationality. But before one goes on to stereotype and vilify a nation or its people, one must spend some time critically examining the trends of online sexual harassment of women across the world. Only when we truly understand the current human behavior across the globe, we will be in a far better position to be able to find effective solutions for such problems.

For example:

a) In Europe, 11 per cent of women have experienced inappropriate advances on social websites or have been subjected to sexually explicit emails or text (SMS) messages. 20 per cent of young women (18-29) have been victims of such cyber harassment (FRA 2014).
b) What is even more disturbing is that 16 per cent of Europeans think that sending 'unwanted' sexually explicit emails or messages should not be against the law (Special Eurobarometer 449).

The inappropriate behavior is not just limited to smartphones.

For instance, in Sweden, it was revealed that 4.1 per cent of men and 2.1 per cent of women had revealed their genitals to a stranger at least once in their lives, and quite disturbingly, the act made them sexually aroused (Långström, N, & Seto, MC 2006. Exhibitionistic and voyeuristic behaviour in a Swedish national population survey).

In the western world, the exhibitionistic behaviour of flashing genitals or breasts is not new. Numerous festivals across the western world are held regularly where such activities are promoted and normalised. WoodStock Festival, for instance, many attend these festivals with an objective to get laid and get drunk.

For instance, Mardi Gras – a festival which is associated with Christian tradition also consists of new behaviours in which 'exposed body parts, public sex acts, and flashed breasts, buttocks, and penises are commonplace in many of the parade areas'.[21]

Researchers have studied the behavior of drunken promiscuity in Mardi Gras. 42 per cent of men who attend Mardi Gras expect to have sex with somebody they meet at the festival. '68 per cent of the men and 63 per cent of the women reported having at least five or six drinks per sitting. Almost one-quarter of the men reported having at least 16 drinks per sitting; 15 per cent of women reported the same', says the Milhausen study. Obscene exposure, and exhibitionistic and voyeuristic behavior in the western population are on display in such festivals. The question is: how do we know that in such festivals some participants do not suffer from 'Exhibitionistic Disorder'?

21 A Theory-Based Approach to Understanding Sexual Behavior at Mardi Gras, Robin R Milhausen.

Women in America face a lot of sexual harassment in public transportation every day. More than 1 in 4 women in Washington DC, United States, have experienced some form of sexual harassment (groping 21 per cent, leering 42 per cent, being rubbed against 30 per cent, up-skirt photos 13 per cent) on public transportation. Quite disturbingly, 77 per cent of victims never reported the incident and even more disturbingly 53 per cent of bystanders never reported the behaviour or incident, reports the Washington Metropolitan Area Transit Authority 2016, 2018.

Quite worryingly, 41 per cent of Europeans think that making sexually suggestive comments or 'jokes' to a woman in the street should not be against the law (41 per cent) and 18 per cent say touching a colleague in an unwanted or inappropriate way, should not be illegal (Special Eurobarometer 449).

Killing for love?

The isolated incidents of honour killings (of daughters and sometimes sons by families) in India do end up on international tabloids right away but quite often such stories fail to cover a broader global perspective.

Honour killings in India or elsewhere are indeed as condemnable as the cases of parricide in America.

Kathleen M Heide, PhD who has published multiple books on juvenile homicide is a licensed mental health counselor and an expert in matters related to homicide.

According to her, almost five parents are killed by their biological children in the USA every week. Further studies need to be done to investigate the reason behind such human behaviour – whether it is parents killing children for falling in love, or children killing parents for the reason that they were denied love.

Promiscuous behavior in western societies

Multiple studies have shown that people living in the western nations usually have the largest number of sex partners, far ahead than what it is in a country like India (The Durex Survey 2005, Britain is among casual sex capitals of the western world, *The Telegraph*).

Promiscuous behaviour is also related to sexual abuse during childhood (AAETS report, USA).

The behaviour of having multiple sex partners is not backed by science. It causes serious health and socio-economic effects.

No amount of protection can guarantee safe sex. Viruses and bacteria that causes STDs can even be transmitted through tiny cuts in mouths. In America, 'half of all new STDs reported each year are among young people 15 to 24', says the CDC's Sexually Transmitted Disease Surveillance 2016.

From overuse and side effects to contraceptive pills to teenage pregnancy and labour complications, the effects of promiscuous behavior can be very detrimental to any society.

In America, CDC data shows that in 2017, among US high school students, '40 per cent had ever had sexual intercourse, seven per cent had been physically forced to have sexual intercourse when they did not want to, 10 per cent had four or more sexual partners, 46 per cent did not use a condom the last time they had sex, 14 per cent did not use any method to prevent pregnancy, 19 per cent had drunk alcohol or used drugs before last sexual intercourse and less than 10 per cent of all students have ever been tested for human immunodeficiency virus (HIV)'.

Are youngsters in developing nations like India aware of where they are heading while adopting the western sexualised cultures without any critical examination?

The overall moral breakdown in western society has hurt many lives. In particular, the situation is more alarming in the homes with broken families.

These failed western experiments that have led to its damaged social fabric should be studied by the nations and countries which are still not in a very advanced stage of adopting western cultural models. While doing this, the idea should not be to shame any country, culture or peoples but to understand human behaviour and to find out the factors that have caused psychologically damaged minds and psychologically damaged societies.

This becomes even more important as such is the impact of the mighty soft power of the former colonial powers and many western nations, that on many occasions, it appears that developing nations tend to blindly search for readymade western solutions for their existing problems without any critical examination. As a result, not only they end up bringing the failed foreign experiments to their countries, but also, they are not able to protect and preserve the best practices that they already have. The western nations with their broken family institution and highly sexualised atmosphere cannot be the global role models when it comes to fighting with the menace of sexual crimes.

TEN

WHAT INDIA COULD LEARN FROM THE WEST

INDIA'S GROWING economic might may sound very impressive, but very frustratingly, India has not managed to fix some of the very basic things, and some of those things are in a hapless state. Most of these things require no import of technology from any country, and having them will not only transform the way India looks but it will also make the country a lot more habitable.

Pavements and bicycle tracks: A proper pavement infrastructure is something that India needs desperately. This is one simple thing which requires no special technology but can deliver many benefits. Proper pavements will encourage more urban Indians to walk to work. An increase in the number of women on pavements should improve the sense of safety. Activities like jogging, skateboarding, and cycling will reduce vehicular traffic, improve fitness, and the streets will start to look more organised. Mothers will be able to freely use baby strollers and the disabled will no longer struggle with their wheelchairs.

Yes, something as simple as pavements can reduce fuel consumption and number of deaths due to jaywalking.

Differently abled (Disabled) friendly infrastructure: India has millions of differently abled (disabled) people. Every day many of them struggle, as in most places India's public infrastructure is not disabled-friendly. Even most private buildings and properties lack that facility. Shouldn't India try to add more convenience to the lives of disabled people?

Air ambulances: India has some of the worst traffic jams in the world. But it does not have a proper air ambulance infrastructure. Why? In a country of more than 1.3 billion, imagine how many lives can be saved every day if the patients can be taken to hospital faster.

Poor management of construction sites: By 2021, India is expected to overtake Japan to become the world's third largest construction market (Global Construction 2030).

This seems impressive, but India's management of its construction sites largely remains poor. The construction sites in India are one of the sources of particulate matter emissions which is already a very big problem in many parts of India. Additionally, a lack of safety gear and personal protective equipment (PPE) for the workers remains a big problem.

Chaotic electric wires: India should try to get rid of these hanging electric cables. They look ugly and pose a big danger.

Potholes on Indian roads: China and Russia have a high rate of death by road accidents. Unfortunately, India is slightly ahead of them, says the global status report on road safety 2018, WHO.

Many of these deaths in India can be avoided if the potholes are repaired fast enough.

The Indian government has been constructing millions of toilets, and the WHO has praised its efforts. However, there is something more which should be addressed, and that is clean toilets on the highways. In Europe, most fuel stations have paid (or free) clean toilets which are very convenient. What is stopping the fuel stations in India from building something similar?

Frequently, I notice that Indian roads and highways are still being swept manually. How efficient can that be? Why does India not replace that with road vacuum cleaning trucks for faster and better results?

India should also speed up the process of cleaning its rivers; it should fix its drainage and sewage system and it should really do something to preserve its architectural sites better.

So far, the things that I have mentioned require efforts by the government. But there is a lot that the common citizens in India can do on their own.

First and foremost, waste segregation: Yes, in per capita terms, India produces far less waste than the western nations. But, why is waste segregation at its source not common practice in India? In a country where waste management is a big problem, this is something that citizens can do to make things easier for the government.

Indians should also learn how to respond faster to give the right of passage to an ambulance.

They can also learn the art of queuing from the British. Is there any other country who does it better than Britain?

Indians can become more punctual. They can also develop a habit of holding the door open for strangers.

In the southern region of India, I have noticed that the houses are painted better. Well-painted homes help in improving the cityscapes.

Habits like littering or tobacco spitting should be stopped.

In the early 19th-century, the American habit of spitting tobacco juice disgusted many British visitors. Charles Dickens called Washington 'the head-quarters of tobacco-tinctured saliva'. Gradually the practice declined in the USA. (American Notes for General Circulation, Charles Dickens.)

However, in India this practice is not completely dead yet.

In India, people expect public toilets to be clean, but as long as their own toilets at home are dirty, it appears to be an impossible task.

Can you imagine a country with clean public toilets but dirty home toilets? I can't. From my personal experience, I can say that most home toilets in the West are as clean as they are in the five-star hotels of India. The clean toilet culture in India has to start from homes; only then will it reach the public places.

It is not just about the condition of toilets in homes; if you take a flight with a lot of Indian passengers on it, the situation gets pretty bad in the airplane's lavatory too.

And how about learning some other airplane etiquette?

Most Indians do not like waiting. Line jumping is almost normal behaviour. When the airplane reaches its destination, they want to be the first to alight from the plane. Even if you are seated at the first row, it might be possible that you are the last one to leave the plane, unless you are ruthless enough to push yourself through the line. It doesn't matter if you are a female or if you are carrying a baby. Even fellow females will hardly care.

At least 20 students were killed when a fire engulfed a coaching center in a commercial building in Surat. The building had no fire escape. Poor fire safety in India is a very serious concern. Most buildings lack that.

India does not have a child safety seat culture. In general, people in India are not even aware of the benefits of child safety seats. In Europe and America, it is an offence if children are not seated and buckled in a proper car seat. When will India implement a similar law? People don't really need to wait for the government to bring in legislation: Learn about car seats, get the right one for your child and start using it.

CPR (cardio pulmonary resuscitation) is a life-saving procedure, but most Indians have no clue about it. A survey conducted in 20 Indians cities revealed that only 3 per cent of people know the CPR technique (Lybrate). Now, if that is the situation in the Indian cities, imagine what it could be like in Indian villages. In a country, where ambulances hardly make it on time, knowledge of the CPR technique among citizens becomes even more important.

In India, there is some sort of disconnect between citizens and government. A survey found that 70 per cent of Indian youths was not aware about the government-run skill development programmes that may benefit them.[1]

India has two million street food vendors, says the Ministry of Urban Poverty Alleviation, GoI.

The country has mouthwatering street food which is generally quite fresh and is loved by people of all income groups. In addition, it provides self-employment opportunities to the economically disadvantaged, and is a major source of nutrition for the low-middle class and urban poor.

---

1 Young India and Work by the Observer Research Foundation and World Economic Forum.

But is the Indian street food always hygienic?

The Food Safety and Standards Authority of India (FSSAI) has launched a national campaign to improve the hygiene practices and safety standards of food vendors. Across the country, 144 street food clusters have been identified which will be jointly audited with state authorities for hygiene and cleanliness. In 2018, Ahemdabad's Kankaria Lake area became India's first Clean Street Food Hub (Project Clean Street Food, FSSAI).

These are good signs, but India has a long way to go to match the standards in Europe or America.

If you want to purchase or rent a new property in India, you may notice the poor finishing or lack of attention to detail. Brand new apartments in India already look worn out and aged, at least by European standards. Why?

Is it because Indians tend to compromise easily, or is it because of the fact that India's low-skilled labourers are not professionally trained?

The situation is also pretty bad when it comes to the management of government's offices and hospitals. Most of them are not properly maintained. I am often told that it used to be even worse. Citizens should be held equally responsible. I do not think that the Indian government can fix any of these things without proper participation by citizens.

When it comes to Indian government employees, you do not see the kind of discipline and professionalism that you see in their counterparts in Europe or America.

In most European countries, there is not much difference between the quality of a public school in a village or one in a city. But in India, students in the villages are very disadvantaged.

Even China is doing a lot better. A NITI Aayog 2019 study revealed that '...India has almost 3-4 times the number of schools (1.5 million) than China (0.5 million) despite a similar population'. But the quality of Indian schools is worse.

Nearly 400,000 Indian schools '...have less than 50 students each and a maximum of two teachers'. In rural India, the student-to-teacher ratio can be as bad as one teacher to 100-plus students (NITI Aayog).

Many Indians are very proud of their spiritual heritage and have lots of respect for their places of worship. Spiritual tourism is economically very important for the country. But most Indian cities which have spiritual significance remain extremely dirty. Tirupati in the southern part of India is one of the exceptions.

On the other hand, in the West, the places of worship and the places which have religious importance are in immaculate condition.

India wants to fix its poor waste management infrastructure and it wants to clean its rivers, but the progress is very slow. Why? What is stopping India from investing money to fix its waste management issues? Won't it create more jobs? Won't it help India to save in health care costs and help the economy, as more tourists will be encouraged to come to India?

Some Indians could also have more confidence in their identity, languages and cultural heritage. Yes, post-colonial identity crisis is not too easy to handle, but attempts should be made to empower those who have low confidence.

It is in India's interest to preserve the best that it has, and to bring the best that it can find outside its borders.

Yes, there are things that India can learn from the West.

Should India follow the West blindly?

It is important to construct a society that is not hesitant to learn the best global practices, but in the process, it is also important that the failed socioeconomic experiments and practices from foreign countries are not blindly imported. FASD is an issue that I personally find very sensitive. Something really needs to be done before everything is completely and permanently lost.

Alcohol consumption and FASD

The blind race to follow the western lifestyle has made many people feel that Indian women are backward because they don't drink like western women do.

European countries have a very high prevalence of alcohol use during pregnancy. For instance, about 60 per cent of Irish women drink during pregnancy. In the UK, it is 41 per cent and in Denmark, it is 46 per cent.[2]

In the western world, alcohol consumption during pregnancy is a major public health concern.

Government health organisations in countries like the USA, the UK, Canada and Australia have already issued guidelines which say that no amount of alcohol (wine, beer, liquor etc.) is safe for pregnant women (CDC, USA). Drinking alcohol during pregnancy can cause serious harm to the developing foetus 'resulting in CNS and physical damage' which has 'several lifelong health consequences'.This damage can lead to foetal alcohol spectrum disorder or FASD, which is an umbrella term that covers all the various effects that a child may sustain if their mothers drink alcohol during pregnancy. FASD includes

---

2 Estimation of national, regional, and global prevalence of alcohol use during pregnancy and fetal alcohol syndrome: a systematic review and meta-analysis – Svetlana Popova, Shannon Lange, Charlotte Probst, Gerrit Gmel, Jürgen Rehm.

foetal alcohol syndrome (FAS), partial FAS, and alcohol-related neurodevelopmental disorder (Comorbidity of fetal alcohol spectrum disorder: a systematic review and meta-analysis).

European countries like Britain, Italy, Croatia, Belarus and Ireland have a very high rate of foetal alcohol syndrome and the prevalence of FAS is the highest in the WHO European Region (37.4 per 10 000 people, 95 per cent CI 24.7–54.2).[3]

More disturbingly, 'It is common for individuals with FASD to be involved in inappropriate sexual behaviours (ISB)'.[4]

Secondary conditions also involve mental health problems, disrupted school experience, trouble with the law and problems with alcohol and drugs (CDC).

Additionally, the risk of FASDs in children is significantly higher in various child care systems (Prevalence of Alcohol Consumption during Pregnancy and Fetal Alcohol Spectrum Disorder, Svetlana (Lana) Popova, MD, PhD, MPH, Centre for Addiction and Mental Health, University of Toronto).

For any nation, the costs of drinking alcohol during pregnancy can be painfully large. For instance, in Canada, the annual financial burden of FASD was estimated at 1.8 billion Canadian Dollars (The Burden and Economic Impact of Fetal Alcohol Spectrum Disorder in Canada, Svetlana Popova Principal Investigator, Shannon Lange, Larry Burd and Jurgen Rehm).

---

3 Estimation of national, regional, and global prevalence of alcohol use during pregnancy and fetal alcohol syndrome: a systematic review and meta-analysis – Svetlana Popova, Shannon Lange, Charlotte Probst, Gerrit Gmel, Jürgen Rehm.

4 FASD and Inappropriate Sexual Behaviour Tara Anderson,a,b Kelly D Harding, a, c Dorothy Reid, a Jacqueline Peia,daCanada FASD Research Network, bUniversity of Saskatchewan, c Laurentian University, dUniversity of Alberta.

In 2010, a survey was conducted in Europe on behalf of the European Commission. It revealed that 88 per cent of women totally agreed or tended to agree that alcohol could cause birth defects (Prevention of harm caused by alcohol exposure in pregnancy).

But this doesn't stop the western women from consuming alcohol.

Whether it is a social gathering or just relaxing, alcohol is an essential part of the western lifestyle.

According to a study, in the 27 countries of the European Union, 82.1 per cent of women were current drinkers. (Modeling the impact of alcohol dependence on mortality burden and the effect of available treatment interventions in the European Union. Rehm J, Shield KD, Gmel G, Rehm MX, Frick U.)

In India, just 1.2 per cent of women drink alcohol(NFHS 4).

It is not too difficult to understand that a high consumption of alcohol in the western nations is also related to the economic interests of the western alcohol industry.

The National Institutes of Health (NIH) is America's medical research agency and it is a part of the US Department of Health and Human Services. Its 'controversial' study that was supposed to find out whether moderate drinking has health benefits was terminated after it was reported that the study was being funded by the alcohol industry (Roni Caryn Rabin, NYTimes). Funding of scientific research and studies by the alcohol industry to change or influence the result and to create a perception in public that 'alcohol is healthy' should be totally unacceptable.

One of the fundamental thoughts behind human rights activism is to strengthen the voices of those whose voices are weak. One of the ideas behind animal rights activism is to protect those who do not have a voice.

But are we ready to raise our voices for those babies who are exposed to alcohol in their mother's womb? Is giving voice to these voiceless innocent lives progressive enough? Can it pass as a progressive thought for those who are pretending to be at the forefront of fighting injustice and discrimination?

Yes, women have the right to decide for themselves, but should we forget that the newborn babies also have a right to be born without the disorders that are caused by drinking alcohol during pregnancy? Or should we forget that the foetus also has a right not to consume alcohol?

Yes, it is important for Indians to have the freedom to decide for themselves, but it is equally important for them to be well-informed about the negative consequences of the western commercial monoculture.

Yes, it is important for Indians to modernise and prosper, but it is equally important for them to not become victims of the selfish economic interests of the commercial industries which are funding the scientific research and studies.

India needs many reforms and it should fix its system wherever it is broken. It should not shy away from learning the best global practices, but should India blindly replace all its beautiful traditions with the failed western experiments?

While India was freely sharing its intellectual heritage and its traditions of ayurveda and yoga with the West and was busy healing minds and bodies in the western nations, the West was exporting its commercial monoculture to India. No, it does not mean that in India men and women were not dancing together before. No, it does not mean that men and women were not singing together before. Indians did produce soul-touching music and rhythms, and they did have music concerts in which the attendees would feel high by spiritual awakening, not by alcohol.

Only time will tell whether Indians will stay radiant, colourful and spiritual, or whether they will be de-individualised to become featureless imitations with lost identities.

In its true sense, gender equality never meant that women should also commit the same number of crimes that men commit, and drink the same amount of alcohol that men do.

The practice of drinking alcohol during pregnancy is a very serious social, economic and public health issue that has been bleeding the western nations.

The practice of drinking alcohol during pregnancy is not backed by science. It hurts economic development and it destroys social structure. So, is it right to say that drinking during pregnancy is a backward practice?

ELEVEN

WEST DOMINANT IN GLOBAL BATTLE OF SOFT POWER

Can the real India be discovered?

IT IS quite reasonable to say that the world may never be able to discover the real India or fully benefit from the thoughts, perspectives and the solutions that Indians are able to bring for our global problems unless India starts to rank similar to the western nations in terms of soft power. In the current globalised scenario, in which our world faces a mighty presence of western countries' soft power, the biggest question is: Can You discover the real India?

Why is India so vulnerable to foreign soft power?

It is easier to manipulate a society where a large population suffers from a post-colonial identity crisis resulting in a lot of self-doubt and low self-esteem. The foreign influencers and exploiters understand very well that people who suffer from low self-esteem and low confidence are more likely to adopt foreign cultures, ideologies and lifestyles while giving up their own identity and heritage. This situation opens multiple ways to exploit and conquer such vulnerable societies through religion or commerce.

Capturing global markets through cultural domination is an old and time-tested strategy and the oppressed nations are likely to become socio-culturally, economically and emotionally colonised.

Are these painful stories not important enough?

Numerous disturbing facts and statistics about so many western nations are not always well-known globally. The mighty soft power of western nations doesn't easily let such stories surface in the mainstream.

As a result, the global community misses an opportunity to learn from the experiences of the western nations and the West itself fails to completely benefit from the solutions that the global community can provide to their problems.

For instance, how many of us know that:

In the United States, 41 million people struggle with hunger and that includes 13 million children(USDA Year: 2016).

In Britain, more than 8 million people are living in food poverty and that is close to 13 per cent of the country's population(UN). An estimated 870,000 children in England are regularly going to bed hungry because their parents are not able to provide the meals they need (The Felix Project).

How many of us know that due to hunger, children in the UK are forced to eat toilet paper and scavenge trash bins at night for food? But this is a fact, says Laurence Guinness, chief executive of the Childhood Trust.

Are these heartbreaking stories not important enough? Has the western media done enough to highlight them?

Have you also wondered why white people are considered 'expats' when more often than not, everybody else is considered an immigrant? 'Africans are immigrants. Arabs are immigrants. Asians are immigrants. However, Europeans are expats because they can't be at the same level as other ethnicities' Mawuna Remarque Koutonin notes in *The Guardian*. Is it fair to say that such discriminatory behaviours tend to get normalised due to the overwhelming soft power of the western nations?

Will you still be surprised if I also mention that humiliating 'virginity-tests' were performed upon migrant Indian subcontinent women by the British immigration control officers?[1]

A poll commissioned by Amnesty International revealed shocking results in the UK. It disclosed that '(30 per cent) said that a woman was partially or totally responsible for being raped if she was drunk, (26 per cent) of those asked said that they thought a woman was partially or totally responsible for being raped if she was wearing sexy or revealing clothing', 'Sexual Assault Research', published in 2005, (21 November) said.

The systematic brainwashing by the western media has gone to an extent that a vast majority of the British population is not properly familiar with the actual situation. Many Britishers are not only unable to fully understand the complex layers of a nation like India, but are also unaware of what is happening in their own country.

This situation was clearly evident in the results of the poll which revealed 'that the vast majority of the British population

1 (This atrocitywas exposed in the late 1970's.) National Archives, London (hereafter NA), HO 418/29 338797, letter from Mr Hillary to Mr Flesher, 1February 1979.

has no idea how many women are raped every year in the UK, with 96 per cent of those polled saying they either didn't know the true extent of rape or that they thought it was far lower than the true figure', according to an Amnesty International report.

Such is the level of brainwashing of the general British public that (34 per cent) of the Britishers would like it if Britain still had an empire (YouGov survey).

Well, do they even know that the British empire was responsible for millions of deaths, many atrocities and for the loot of $45 trillion from India during the period 1765 to 1938?[2]

Very sad and shocking indeed!

Another survey found out that one quarter of British people acknowledged that they were racist, according to a British Attitudes Survey.

Will you be surprised, if I mention that 30 per cent of employees in the UK have witnessed or experienced racial harassment in the workplace first-hand in the last twelve months from the date they were surveyed? (Race at Work Report, 2015.)

We all have read numerous media articles praising the so-called 'Scandinavian model' when it comes to the environment. But when a major WWF study criticised Sweden for its unsustainable consumption of the planet's resources, did that news reach to you too? The study revealed that if everyone lived the lifestyles that Swedes do, we would require 4.2 Earths (WWF Living Planet Report, 2016).

How many of us know that the USA which is sitting many places above India in the World Happiness Index (a metric which

---

2 A research by Utsa Patnaik, Published by Columbia University Press. stroke-slash – Inglorious Empire.

does feel outdated) has been struggling to keep its population 'happy' as rates of depression have been rising consistently?[3]

No, it is not only about the claim that they are better diagnosed, as suicidal attempts have been rising as well.[4]

'In 2017, an estimated 10.6 million adults in America, aged 18 or older had thought seriously about trying to kill themselves (4.3 per cent of adults), 3.2 million had made suicide plans (1.3 per cent), and 1.4 million made nonfatal suicide attempts (0.6 per cent)', says the 2017 National Survey on Drug Use and Health, USA.

In 2010, depression had an economic burden of $210.5 billion in the USA (CDC).

'In 2017, 30.5 million people aged 12 or older used an illicit drug in the past 30 days (i.e., current use), which corresponds to about 1 in 9 Americans (11.2 per cent)', the Drug Use Survey adds. Illicit drug usage, bullying, mental health problems, risky behaviour that includes sexual risk and illicit drug usage are all co related, says the 2007-2017 report of the Youth Risk Behaviour Survey Data Summary & Trends. Will an average Indian be able to do a critical examination of these lesser known western sociocultural elements which often stay under the rug due to the humongous soft power of western nations?

---

3 Age, Period, and Cohort Trends in Mood Disorder Indicators and Suicide Related Outcomes in a Nationally Representative Dataset, 2005–2017, American Psychological Association.

4 Field, MD3 Suicidal Attempts and Ideation Among Children and Adolescents in US Emergency Departments, 2007-2015 Brett Burstein, MDCM, PhD, MPH1; Holly Agostino, MDCM2; Brian Green.

Foreign media's strange ways of reporting India

Selective use of per capita metrics

Western media loves to calculate India's GDP in a per capita basis but it frequently forgets to use per capita metrics when it comes to India's rape numbers.

Isn't it strange that the western media, which is the champion of using per capita metrics in their analysis when it comes to India's GDP, are often noticed calculating the rape numbers and carbon emissions in their own countries in absolute numbers?

Well, it is quite understandable why the western nations shy away from calculating their emission on a per capita basis. In per capita terms, even in the case of PM2.5, they are far more polluting than many developing nations which are often criticised for their bad PM2.5 situation.

Even with their tiny population, many western nations are ahead in nitrogen dioxide emissions in both ways (emissions in per capita terms as well as in absolute terms). And how about calculating historical emissions on a per capita basis? How about talking about the consumption-based emissions in per capita terms? Can western scholars and western media also stress that more regularly?

Foreign media's fabricated content and anti-India approach

How many of us know that BBC has a history of publishing fabricated content? In 2011, in an extremely embarrassing situation, the BBC had to apologise for a faked footage of child labour in its show 'Primark: On The Rack' which was broadcast in June 2008. The show involved a Bangalore scene.

Not only that, the BBC had even won the prestigious 'Current Affairs Home Prize at the Royal Television Society Awards' for that programme, (Primark: On The Rack); an award which it later returned.

In 2012, the BBC referred to the Hindu festival of Holi as a 'filthy festival'. Again, it later issued an apology (W Rorrkychand Singh).

Alasdair Pinkerton has done extensive research in the areas of critical geopolitics, media, and the contested geopolitics of 'public diplomacy'. In his research, he has observed the systematic pattern of propagandic and biased coverage of India by the BBC after the country's independence.

'During the early summer of 1970 (10 June), the BBC broadcast the UK premiere of 'Calcutta', a documentary film by acclaimed French director Louis Malle, on British television.'

The film maligned India's image to such an extent that in August 1970, the government of India decided to expel the BBC from India (52 Lok Sabha Debates, Fourth Series, XLIV(22); New Delhi, 1970; 204–226).

'The BBC's British employees were instructed to leave the country, the offices in New Delhi were closed, and locally engaged staff were released from their BBC contracts.' Before the BBC was expelled, the then-Indian High Commissioner had 'warned the BBC's Director General (Sir Charles Curran), that the functioning of the BBC representative in India would become 'superfluous' if such programmes continued to 'vitiate the minds of the British people against India'.

Shashi Bhushan was an Indian freedom fighter and a social worker who participated in the Quit India movement.

Concluding his parliamentary statement, he said:

'The BBC is not only acting against India, but is preaching a new kind of imperialism. They want to re-impose imperialism on

India as they are doing in Angola and Mozambique.'[5]

In an ideal world, we expect the big media houses to do a fair job. Many feel that, just like common citizens, it is natural for journalists to carry some bias in their work. But publishing fake content like the BBC did in Primark's case is completely unacceptable. In such cases, an apology doesn't completely reverse the damage as it doesn't quite reach the very people who consumed the fake content and already based their opinions on that.

BBC's documentary – *India's daughter* created a big controversy in India. Well, nobody could properly highlight that the biased ways of the BBC didn't go completely unnoticed back in England too.

Christopher John Penrice Booker (1937 – 2019) was an English journalist, author and a founder of the satirical magazine *Private Eye*.

He stated:

'If there is a cultural problem here (in the UK), it is the longstanding desire of the western media to stereotype Indian males as sexual predators.'

He added:

'Those who saw the preview of *India's Daughter* in Delhi have testified that the original version did make comparisons with the rest of the world. One, Anna Vetticad, praised it as a "balanced documentary", because it ended with "worldwide statistics highlighting violence against women from Australia to the US". But when the final version emerged, all this had been cut out. India was shown standing alone, as a country where rape is an exceptional problem.'

5 A new kind of imperialism? The BBC, cold war broadcasting and the contested geopolitics of south Asia, Alasdair Pinkerton.

How is western stereotyping hurting India?

How Indians are perceived is directly related to their well-being and safety overseas.

There is no denying that negative stereotyping can lead to hate crimes and discrimination.

Because of the media generated 'rapist' tag on Indian males, a Leipzig University professor – Sickinger – barred an Indian student from an internship on the grounds that 'we hear a lot about the rape problem in India, which I cannot support' (Christopher John Penrice Booker).

Eventually, the German ambassador to India had to intervene.

In his letter to Professor Sickinger, he wrote:

'It has been brought to my attention that you denied an internship to a male Indian student, giving "the rape problem in India" as a reason. Let me make it clear at the outset that I strongly object to this.'

'The 2012 Nirbhaya rape case has refocused attention on the issue of violence against women. Rape is indeed a serious issue in India as in most countries, including Germany. In India, the Nirbhaya case has triggered a lively honest, sustained and very healthy public debate – a public debate of a quality that wouldn't be possible in many other countries. The Indian Government and Indian civil society organisations are very committed to tackling the issue.

'Yesterday we celebrated International Women's Day at the German Embassy here in Delhi with many local activists including many men. Your oversimplifying and discriminating generalisation is an offense to these women and men ardently committed to furthering women's empowerment in India; and it is an offense to millions of law-abiding, tolerant, open-minded and hard-working Indians. Let's be clear: India is not a country of rapists.'

In addition, the way both Indians and India are perceived and understood globally is directly related to the country's trade and tourism opportunities.

Tourism in India serves all sections of society including those who are at the bottom of the economic pyramid. Killing India's tourism opportunities directly hurts India's poor and the country's overall job and wealth generating opportunities.

Furthermore, self-loathing people with low self-esteem and self-confidence cannot be expected to be at their creative best, especially in a country where many are already suffering from the post-colonial identity crisis.

Let's be honest – can we expect earth-shaking revolutionary ideas from those who suffer from inferiority complex and low confidence?

It doesn't mean that India shouldn't find solutions for its existing problems. But then, it also doesn't mean that Indians shouldn't be allowed to have a broader global perspective so that they are better equipped to learn from the experiences and the failed experiments of other nations.

No problem should be blown out of the proportion. In an increasingly globalised world, a careful examination of a problem with a broader global perspective is necessary.

We shouldn't forget that over-estimation or under-estimation of a problem can be equally dangerous. In both cases, one is unlikely to find the most effective solution.

From losing out on the potential revenue-generating opportunities in trade and tourism to the general self-image and self-confidence of an Indian who lives in India or abroad, the general perception of India has its serious socioeconomic effects.

Study abroad: a dream for many Indians

On the other hand, one of the most successful demonstration of the soft power of western nations can be seen in the way the western universities are able to convince Indian parents to send their child abroad for higher studies. Yes, it is true that in a globalised world, there should be no restriction that keeps anybody from studying abroad.

There is also no denying that developing nations should continue to improve their education infrastructures. But the biggest question that arises is: Are Indian parents who are so keen to send their child abroad for education, educated enough themselves about all sides of college life in the western nations? How many Indian parents know that:

A) In the UK, many students are forced to turn to prostitution to make ends meet. One in 10 students use their bodies to make money when they are short of funds, says the National Student Money Survey, UK. Another report by the NUS confirmed that rising tuition fees and living costs are the reason that students are turning to sex work. What is even more troublesome is that nearly half of those who do sex work feel 'very uncomfortable' going to the police to report sexual violence at the hands of clients (NSU).

   The attitude of having sex for money is not completely unusual in the UK.

   A survey found that a total of 42 per cent of Britons would at least consider having sex for money if the money offered was large enough.[6]

B) In the UK, it was found in 2017, that a total of 64 per cent of girls aged 13-21 had experienced sexual harassment or sexual violence at college or school in the past twelve months. It included 39 per cent having their bra strap pulled by a boy and 27 per cent having their skirts pulled up within the last week, according to a report by Girlguiding's Girls' Attitudes Survey.

Nearly three-quarters (71 per cent) of all 16 to18-year-olds (boys and girls) say they hear sexual name-calling with terms such as 'slut' or 'slag' used towards girls at schools on a daily basis or a few times a week. This data is from End Violence Against Women Poll Results for October 2010.

C) A report from the Australian Human Rights Commission revealed that 51 per cent of students were sexually harassed in 2016.

D) In the USA, 80 per cent of college rapes and sexual assaults go unreported to police (US Department of Justice, Office of Justice Programs, Bureau of Justice Statistics).

A study by the Association of American Universities (AAU) revealed chilling details of the extent of sexual abuse in American colleges. 23 per cent of American female college students have experienced some form of unwanted sexual contact, according to the Association of American Universities.

---

6 British sex survey. 1,052 UK adults were interviewed by Opinium Research and the results were weighted to reflect on the profile of all UK adults.

E) In France, a study which was conducted in two major public universities reported that one in five women are victims of sexual assault in college. The source for this information is the 2007 Campus Sexual Assault study.

F) A total of 37 per cent of college students in the USA have used an illicit drug (Stimulants, Benzodiazepines, Opioids, Cannabinoids, Barbiturates) and abused alcohol on a regular basis, reports The National Library of Medicine, National Institutes of Health. A total of 38 per cent of adults in 2017 battled an illicit drug use disorder. In terms of lost workplace productivity, crime-related costs and healthcare expenses, drug abuse and addiction cost American society more than $740 billion annually, says the center on addiction, USA.

G) Four out of five college students in America drink alcohol, says AddictionCenter.com. A total of 37.9 per cent of college students in the age group of 18–22 were involved in binge drinking during the month before the survey (2015 NSDUH).

H) In 2001, in the USA, more than 696,000 (12 per cent) students between the ages of 18 and 24 were assaulted by another student who had been drinking. A total of 97,000 between the ages of 18 and 24 (2 per cent) experienced alcohol-related sexual assault or date rape.[7]

I) Nearly 25 per cent of college students in America report academic consequences from drinking which includes –

7 Magnitude Of Alcohol-Related Mortality And Morbidity Among US College Students Ages 18–24: Changes From 1998 To 2001, Ralph Hingson, Timothy Heeren, Michael Winter, and Henry Wechsler.

> doing poorly on exams or papers, missing class, falling behind in class, and receiving lower grades.[8]

Not only college students, even high school students in America are engaged in various sexually risky behaviours that relate to unintended pregnancies, STIs and HIV infection.

The 2017 national YRBS revealed:

Nearly 10 per cent of high school students in America have had sexual intercourse with four or more people. Among those who were sexually active, more than 45 per cent did not use condoms during their last encounter of sexual intercourse. Quite disturbingly, during the 12 months before the survey, 7.4 per cent of high school students had attempted suicide.

It should be stressed that on many occasions, international students are too afraid or ashamed to speak up when they are targeted. Quite understandably, it may not be easy for them to reveal the true story of their sexual harassments to their parents back home, especially when on many occasions, parents borrow money or sell asset to send their child abroad or in some occasions, children rebel against their parents to go abroad to study in the first place.

Many also fear the risk of getting deported without completing their studies.

A Chinese student studying at the prestigious Australian National University was raped by an Australian student. She said, '...it's the thing you will never tell your parents if it's possible to

---

8 Wechsler, H Dowdall, GW Maenner, G et al. Changes in binge drinking and related problems among American college students between 1993 and 1997: Results of the Harvard School of Public Health College Alcohol Study.

hide it…you are spending their money and coming this far away to study and you got raped. It's disgraceful'.

It should also be mentioned that when the Chinese student went to the Australian police to seek help, the policewoman said, 'don't worry…next time, just be careful' (Australia: Rape on Campus, a documentary film, Al Jazzera).

Are these stories and facts not important enough for the parents in developing countries who on various occasions borrow money from banks and sell their assets to send their child to western nations? Is this information not important for those parents who are keen to relocate or migrate to other countries with their children?

Has the global media done enough to highlight these issues to spread awareness in general public interest?

Worldwide, students must have complete freedom regarding how they want to pursue their career, but shouldn't be everyone well-informed and aware of the complete scenario before they make their decision?

Has the soft power of the western nations blinded us in some way?

Which countries have the highest soft power?

There shouldn't be a surprise that the former colonial power – Britain has the highest soft power in the world. It is followed by France, Germany and the United States. Apart from Japan and Australia (depends on whether you consider Australia a western nation or not) every. Another nation with the highest soft power in the Soft Power 30 Index is from the western world (The Soft Power 30 index, The Soft Power 30, 2018).

Well, thanks to their immense soft power, there shouldn't be any surprise that the nations in the list are generally the nations, which are perceived in a quite positive way globally.

If you feel outraged due to the fact that the British empire was responsible for millions of deaths, violation of human rights, many atrocities and for the loot of $45 trillion from India during the period 1765 to 1938, it doesn't matter (Utsa Patnaik, Shashi Tharoor).

Thanks to its humongous soft power, the UK is generally perceived so well across the world.

With its powerful global presence, the British media house, BBC is a 'valuable soft power asset' for the UK (The Soft Power 30, 2018).

Here is a list of the countries with the highest soft power according to their ranks:

1 United Kingdom
2 France
3 Germany
4 United States
5 Japan
6 Canada
7 Switzerland
8 Sweden
9 Netherlands
10 Australia
11 Denmark
12 Italy
13 Norway
14 Spain
15 Finland

(Source: The Soft Power 30 index, The Soft Power 30, 2018).

What constitutes a nation's soft power?

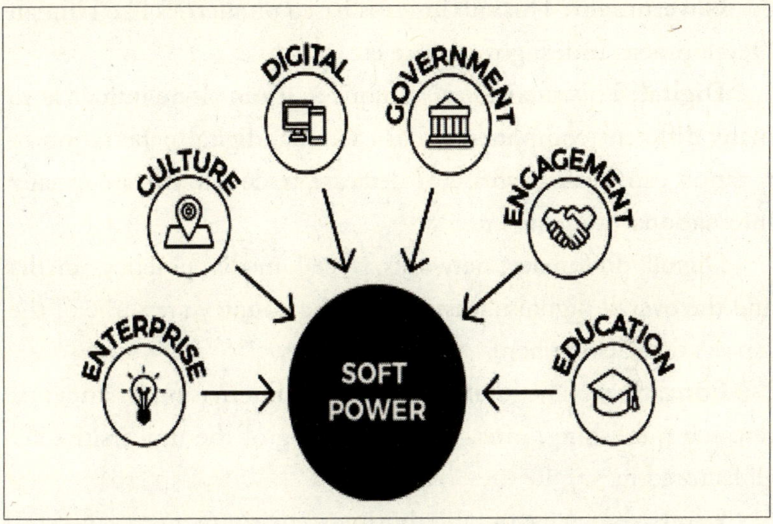

Source: The Soft Power 30 index, The Soft Power 30, 2018

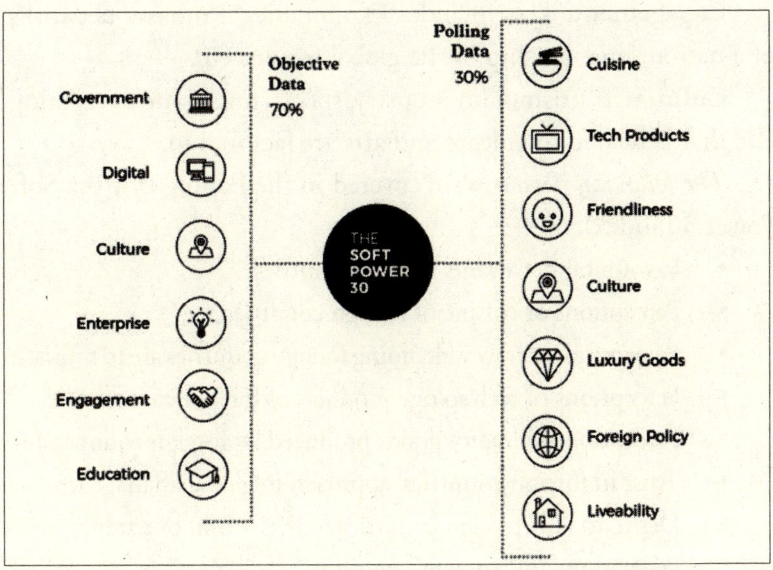

Source: The Soft Power 30 index, The Soft Power 30, 2018

The objective data consists of 6 components (sub-indices):

Government: This sub index is based on metrics like Human Development Index, governance etc.

Digital: This sub index is unique as it can alone influence so many different components. For example, digital penetration of a nation can easily increase or decrease trade / tourism / expat / international students interest.

Digital diplomacy networks, social media potency, media and the overall digital infrastructure in a country are some of the aspects that belong here.

Education: The ability to attract international students, research publishing, international ranking of the universities are all factored in.

Enterprise: A favourable business environment, a country's attractiveness as a business destination are included.

Engagement: This includes Diplomatic / Embassy networks of a nation, membership in the global forums etc.

Culture: Tourism, film industry, sports, music and everything else that is related to culture and arts are factored in.

The following factors were covered in the Polling (for the Soft Power 30 index):

- Favourability towards foreign countries;
- Perceptions of cuisine of foreign countries;
- Perceptions of how welcoming foreign countries are to tourists;
- Perceptions of technology products of foreign countries;
- Perceptions of luxury goods produced by foreign countries;
- Trust in foreign countries' approach to global affairs;
- Desire to visit foreign countries to live, work, or study;
- Perceptions of foreign countries' contributions to global culture.

Nobody should be surprised that India is absent from The Soft Power 30 Index. The report mentioned that the country makes 'remarkably poor use of it' as it 'does not yet benefit as much from international awareness, positive associations, or investments in cultural diplomacy as many other countries',making it an underperformer. In the list of 60 countries, India is ranked at 41st position.

Even among the Asian nations, India sits low at 8th position, below nations like Thailand, Taiwan and Malaysia. Even when we breakdown the six components of the Soft Power 30 index India can't be seen anywhere in the top 10:

Though the index may have some limitations, to an extent, it manages to reflect the overall global situation. The report states: As with every composite index, ours is not without its limitations and shortcomings. The subjective nature of soft power makes comparison across all countries difficult. Moreover, the total complexity of the dynamics of inter-state relations – where soft power is brought to bear – cannot be fully rendered by a comparative global index.

India ranks 35th in Digital, 37th in Government, 38th in culture, 47th in enterprise, 47th in engagement, and 51st in education.

India must continue to invest in its core sectors like education, infrastructure and science. It should also continue its fight against corruption. But, as a developing nation, and with a lower per capita budget, India can't be expected to match the developed nations in various parameters right away. On the other hand, if the soft power assets of the former colonial powers do negative publicity of a formerly colonised nation like India which is trying hard to rebuild and reclaim, its journey to prosperity will only get tougher.

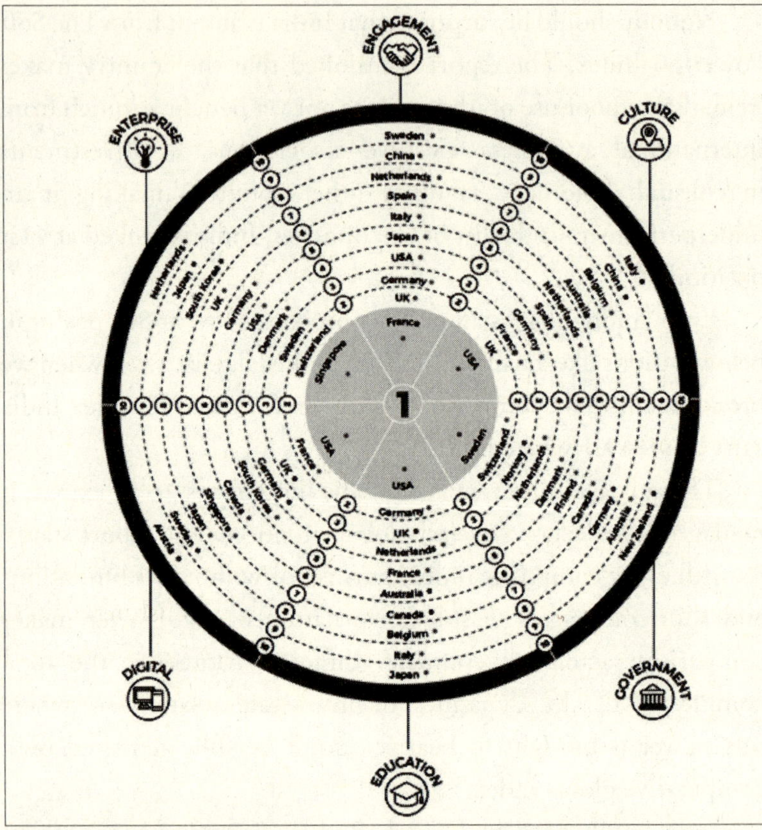

Source: The Soft Power 30 index, The Soft Power 30, 2018

Just having resources is not enough, as it is even more important how a nation utilises them. For example, India may have a big film industry but if its own film industry creates negative stereotypes, then India will not be able to fully utilise that soft power component. Also, if India gives a free hand to foreign soft power assets in form of foreign-owned media which eventually create negative stereotypes by misusing its freedom of journalism, India is likely to lose opportunities in trade and tourism and in many other components resulting in the weakening of its other soft power components and sub-indices.

Furthermore, continuous bashing by the global media is also likely to seriously impact the overall morale of a nation. Can you expect people with low self-confidence and low self-esteem to be at their creative best? If people are not at their creative best, will they be able to find the best solutions for their problems?

Vulnerable and depressed minds are more likely to blindly copy and imitate, and less likely to create and innovate.

It is worth discussing, that even if India overcomes its various challenges and improves its position in sub-indices and other components like Government, Enterprise, Engagement, Education, Tech Products, Luxury Goods, Foreign Policy and Livability will it ever be able to replace the UK, France or USA from their top positions if it can't produce a global media house like the BBC? And even if it does succeed in establishing a global media house, which can penetrate as deeply as BBC has, will it still not continue to be stereotyped by the already 'existing' powerful global digital media houses?

The Digital sub-index of The Soft Power 30 index indicates that India's digital presence is nowhere close to the powerful global penetration of the western nations which they enjoy through their numerous media houses. Of course, the BBC is just one small part of that massive western digital ecosystem. Many western nations have multiple global media houses with the size of viewership and global engagement that the developing nations can only dream of.

As mentioned earlier, the media is extremely important because it (the Digital sub-index of the soft power index) can positively or negatively influence other sub-indices by encouraging or discouraging one's interest in exploring the options in things like culture, tourism, business and education of any nation.

The media component itself is so powerful, that it can enhance other soft power components when it is nicely utilised. India has performed very poorly as far as its overall digital diplomacy network is concerned.

This present situation could also raise a question if the world ever gets to fully know about and learn from the 'failures and experiences of the western nations' or will we just continue to be mesmerised and brainwashed by the glossy cover of the western nations which is fueled by its 'digital diplomacy' and media-enhanced immense soft power?

Tourism doesn't only bring wealth and jobs but also empowers those who are at the bottom of the economic pyramid. What is wrong in promoting a nation's tourism potential in front of the world? Of course, nations do compete for international tourists. For example, If India lose international tourists due to any reason on a particular year, as a result, some other nations will eventually gain additional foreign visitors. Somebody's gain is somebody's loss. It is as simple as that.

'Media coverage of India is often unhelpful and unflattering. Issues like pollution and gender equality consume much of the media oxygen on India' (Soft Power 30 Report).

While we have countries like India, which is perceived far worse than what it actually is we also have countries like France which is perceived far too better than what it actually is. Some international tourists who visit Paris for the first time have to be treated and counselled if they suffer from 'Paris Syndrome'.

Paris Syndrome is a disturbing psychological condition, which is experienced by some tourists and visitors who go to Paris but face extreme shock and trauma at finding out that Paris is far too different from their expectations. The syndrome was identified by a Japanese psychiatrist – Professor Hiroaki Ota.

Psychiatric symptoms such as hallucinations, acute delusional states, feelings of 'being a victim of prejudice', anxiety, vomiting and dizziness etc. are commonly observed in the victims.

Surprised because you heard it for the first time? Well, you shouldn't be! France ranks second in the 2018 Soft Power 30 Index.

Is India's 'soft power' still India's?

While India is struggling to strengthen its core components of soft power, does it even realise that it's so-called own 'soft power' is not completely owned by it anymore? Without even visiting India or knowing India, India's own soft power is being consumed, utilised and exploited by many across the world.

Yoga can be a good example. Across the world, many are practicing yoga without necessarily knowing its Dharmic and Indian roots.

Perhaps, yoga was never supposed to originally act as a soft power as it is more about empowering oneself to unite with the divine. But Yoga increasingly started to be seen as a type of soft power when Americans Americanised it. America has the biggest chunk in the global yoga industry, registration of a yoga school with a renowned USA based organisation adds value to a Yoga school, no matter which part of the world it is in.

India may have a greater number of people practicing yoga, but in proportions it is America which is more likely to come out on top.

It can even be said that if not already, yoga is gradually becoming an American soft power. And the nation from the part of the world where the spiritual practice was originally born is trying to reclaim yoga by its 'better late than never' kind of initiatives like 'International Yoga Day'.

The Americanisation of yoga has also hurt yoga's spiritual Dharmic roots. Yoga's ethos is being diluted right in front of us. Perhaps, the future generations may even claim that yoga originated in the USA.

In the 2016 Yoga in America Study (published in a PDF format) which was conducted by Yoga Journal and Yoga Alliance to understand of the practice of yoga in America and to determine how Americans view yoga, didn't even have 'India' mentioned once in it. Though the study aimed to check how Americans view yoga, it didn't ask the participants any question about its roots or origins. Interestingly, one of the key findings of the study was that: Yoga is an increasing part of 'American life'.

No, I am not suggesting a change in the questions of that study, but as an observer, I find it very interesting that yoga is being discussed, taught, consumed without discussing India or any Indian component. Can India claim today that yoga is its exclusive soft power? Perhaps, it has already lost that opportunity. Is it right to say that yoga is now an American soft power as much as it is India's?

Yoga was supposed to be an important element in the 'culture sub-index' of India. (Refer to the sub-indices of the Soft Power 30 Framework.)

But, is yoga, as a soft power, serving American interest more than India's?

India's dharmic traditions do not believe in the doctrine of global expansion and will never have the same global ambitions as some other religions do. So, when it comes to cultural influence through religion, India will always remain in a disadvantageous position.

India should speed up in the process of improving its fundamentals – from education infrastructure and civic infrastructure to the overall business-friendly environment. It is gradually getting better, but probably not fast enough.

It's a pity that a country which represents nearly one-sixth of the entire mankind has fewer embassies than some nations which have a very little population. An improvement can be demanded there as well.

India has no choice but to fight the negative publicity that surrounds it.

Jonathan McClory, of Soft Power 30 Report, said: 'Global media is rarely helpful when it comes to presentation of India and a lot of that comes down to some of the big issues that they like to just hammer away on so there is an image problem and there is a need for India to tell its side of the story more effectively…'

There is no denying that India has the potential to offer solutions to the current problems (as explained in the chapter, Does India hold the answers to world's problems?) that we are facing globally, but with its weak soft power and its population which is suffering from post-colonial identity crisis, will India be able to reach its true potential? And finally, even if the world wakes up and realises the importance of the Indian idea, will India still be able to claim the ownership of that idea while facing all the appropriation that is happening to its intellectual heritage?

Furthermore, it should also be stressed that the Soft Power 30 index is not an Indian creation. Most of the metrics through which we measure various parameters globally and on which the Soft Power 30 index bases its calculations, are not Indian creation either.

In a way, we are still gauging things with the help of tools, thoughts and perspectives which are not Indian.

Indians also need to discover their own metrics and tools through which they will understand and study global affairs. That's when the world will truly know what the Indian perspective is.

India needs its own versions of HSBC and Citibank, its own version of S&P and Moody's, its own versions of KPMG and PwC, its own social media platforms, its own version of BBC and CNN, its own version of the Oscar and the Nobel, its own highly reputed scientific journals and academic institutions, its own global thinktanks which can influence the investor's sentiment and international policy-making and its own international human right bodies.

And of course, it eventually will need a permanent seat in the UNSC.

Until that happens, India will not be able to cement its rightful place at the global stage and will not be able to fully utilise its soft power to positively impact global affairs.

Give it a thought: Is it too much of a demand that Indians are only asking to be treated with mutual respect from the nations which are developed or are former colonial powers? Believe me, Indians can't wait to experience prosperity too and they are working hard for it. Yes, they make mistakes and they learn from them. What's wrong with that?

India is big, India is diverse and understanding India can be complex, even for Indians, let alone the rest of the world.

Today, India is rebuilding but, in this process, it has its share of vulnerabilities. Many Indians continue to suffer from a post-colonial identity crisis, and they need to be empowered.

Many of them are just innocently ill-informed about the western world. The confidence has fallen so low that for many of them, the West is the shining pillar of all virtues.

In India, many western ideas and practices are blindly imported without any critical examination. India does not have enough dedicated think-tanks which can deeply analyse the global affairs and help Indians in learning the best global practices and also help them in rejecting the failed foreign experiments.

If taken in the right spirit, globalisation can be good, but globalisation does not mean Westernisation or Americanisation.

The people of India have suffered so much economically and culturally by multiple invasions and colonisation. At this vulnerable stage, don't you think that they also deserve some social and cultural independence? Maybe they also need some personal time, so that they can repair what was damaged and can regain their lost identities?

Don't you feel that they also deserve the right to oppose cultural genocide by the foreign monocultures which have homogenised and diluted so many of its beautiful cultures and are still active in so many ways?

Don't you think that India also needs an environment where foreigners don't come to tell them that they are praying to false gods and their gods are 'demons'?[9]

Let us not forget that India is an integral part of our beautiful world. With that perspective, should we not consider India's golden heritage as a valuable global asset? Shouldn't we all come forward to do what we can to preserve it in its authentic form?

Well, it is not just about India's story, in fact, there are so many nations in Africa, Asia and in other parts of the world which must have so much to offer to the world in terms of their traditional wisdom and revolutionary futuristic ideas. But their voices are

---

9 Missouri Megachurch Pastor Condemns Yoga, Calls Hinduism 'Demonic', by Katherine Hignett on 11/13/18, Newsweek / Yoga is 'unsavoury' and 'endangers the soul', Priest Padraig O'Baoill / Pastor Mark Driscoll of Seattle's Mars Hill Church - yoga is 'absolute paganism' and 'demonic'. / Practicing yoga is Satanic, it leads to evil, Gabriele Amorth / Father Roland Colhoun - yoga leads to the 'Kingdom of Darkness' and draws people toward 'Satan and the fallen angels'. (2015).

not easily heard because of the dominance of a few nations in the most powerful international forums. In a globalised world, are we giving equal treatment and an equal opportunity to each and every nation and their people to positively influence our planet? How can the global forums preach equality and pluralism when they themselves are not giving equal opportunities to all nations to participate in them?

Reforms are not only required in many nations but are also required in various global forums.

Without equal participation of all nations and peoples, we as a global society, will never reach our true potential.

Time will pass and eventually India may grow economically, and its citizens may become wealthy, but in this unfair and inadequate global soft-power battle, will India manage to remain India?

TWELEVE

WHO ARE THE ENEMIES OF INDIA'S IDENTITY AND DIVERSITY?

ACTIVISM FOR pluralism cannot be done in a homogenised world. Hypocrisy is dying a thousand deaths every day when many self-proclaimed progressive people are homogenising our world's diversity by their actions which blindly support the western commercial monoculture.

The thought to preserve the cultural heritage is a UN-backed idea which by all accounts is truly liberal and scientific.[1] Then why is it, that on so many occasions, the true protectors and preservers of cultural heritage are considered backward and those who are homogenising our world's diversity and pluralism through western

1 UNESCO's Universal Declaration on Cultural Diversit

commercial and religious monoculture are allowed to present themselves as the messiah of pluralism? The actions of such self-proclaimed progressive people are the true enemies of the global civilizational heritage and our pluralistic and diverse world.

Is it true that the main motivation of such forces which are homogenising our world is to achieve global domination through commerce, religion or through their individual philosophy? Or is it their political motivation – rooted in the desire to rule, not to serve. Or is it through a combination of any or all of these?

Is it true that the idea of global conquest[2] is responsible for homogenisation and for killing the pluralistic attributes of humankind?

It does appear that the idea of global conquest is against the principles on which the United Nations is built upon.

For thousands of years, India has provided an atmosphere that has allowed multiple cultures to flourish, prosper and to celebrate their uniqueness and individual identities. India's diversity and pluralism has attracted its visitors for thousands of years.

But is everything alright with today's India?

Does India have enemies of its diversity? Can India identify them? Can India save itself from them?

Pluralism is a system that encourages the people who wear different clothes, eat different food and speak different languages to live together in harmony. But can pluralism survive, if we do not save diversity?

Have you observed that there are some people who act as

---

2 Islam and Christianity share 'idea of conquest', says Pope Francis, https://www.theguardian.com/world/2016/may/17/pope-francis-islam-christianity-share-idea-of-conquest-sadiq-khan retrieved on 14/6/2019.

the biggest supporters of pluralism but actually, their actions are destroying our diversity?

These self-proclaimed progressive people who often claim to be pro-pluralism want us to wear the same type of clothes, eat the same food and speak the same language, and they are deceitfully turning our beautifully diversified world into a plain and a boring world.

They are imposing their lifestyle and their religions on others, and they are doing everything to make the followers of the native traditions feel backward, uncomfortable, confused and inferior.

With every passing year, India is becoming less and less diverse. Its native cultures and traditions are being diluted. The country that is known for its incredible diversity is gradually losing its most cherished treasure. It is losing its languages, its cultures and even its cuisine. Many Indians have started to feel uncomfortable celebrating their traditional festivals. They are uncomfortable wearing their traditional clothes and speaking their own regional languages. Traditional clothes are even labelled as backward and outdated, and many who wear them are ridiculed. And the irony is that the people who claim to be the biggest advocates of pluralism in India are the people who are making India plain, diluted and boring.

In India, it is estimated that around 220 languages have disappeared in the last 50 years, and another 150 could become extinct in the next five decades. UNESCO's Atlas of the World's Languages in Danger indicates that India has 197 endangered languages, more than any other country in the world.[3]

We are being homogenised, but how many of us notice it?

---

3 UNESCO's Atlas of the World's Languages in Danger.

If the traditional practices are ethical, why should they be ridiculed and looked down upon? Yes, it is possible to benefit from a positive cultural exchange that does not make anyone feel inferior or superior. Yes, it is possible to benefit from science, but it is also important to reject scientific misconduct.

Conversation about ecosystems, species and cultures is extremely important for the continuation of life on Earth. In 2001, UNESCO acknowledged this.

Article 4 of UNESCO's Universal Declaration on Cultural Diversity, stated, 'The defence of cultural diversity is an ethical imperative, inseparable from respect for human dignity'.

Article 1 stated, '...cultural diversity is as necessary for humankind as biodiversity is for nature'. It also recognised cultural diversity as the 'common heritage of humanity...' that '...should be recognised and affirmed for the benefit of present and future generations'.

Isn't it in the interest of the whole humanity that we come forward to preserve India's traditions and its cultural diversity?

The situation is threatening, but all is not lost yet. The problem is global, and India is also a victim. But does India realise that it also has the solution for this problem?

In times such as these, we can benefit from India's foundational wisdom. There is no civilisation in the world which has focused so much on inner exploration; there is no civilisation in the world which has focused so much on conquering one's own mind. It is India's traditional idea that talks about conquering one's own mind and rejects the idea of conquering the world.

The idea of conquering the world is the real enemy of pluralism and diversity. There are many ideologies that have had their entire focus on conquering the world.

India could afford to be so diverse because it has traditionally focused on self-exploration through its Dharmic foundational wisdom. It is India's idea to find the essence of life from within.

The idea to conquer the world has given us violence and hate. It has encouraged people to vilify many native traditions.

It has destroyed our uniqueness and our individual identities. It has caused the cultural and ancestral dislocation of India's native communities.

If we can encourage more people to focus on the inward domain, not only should we be able to reduce all sorts of crimes and wrongdoings globally, but we should also be able to preserve our cultural diversities.

Let us not forget that we need the system of pluralism only because we are diverse. If there is no diversity, there will be no pluralism.

Is it possible that Indians can educate the world about their foundational values and ethos, both of which deal significantly in self exploration?

Across these lines, we could encourage the development of respectful relationships and help many cultures to preserve their dynamism and traditional expressions.

Will India be able to preserve the uniqueness and individuality of its societies and individuals? Will Indians be able to protect their identities from the commercial and religious monoculture?

The problem with many people is that they want to leave their own legacy but are not interested in preserving the legacy that was left for them in form of their own heritage.

And by the way, why should a citizen of a former colonial power decide what an Indian is and what an Indian should be?

India's living cultural heritage

I had an opportunity to spend a lot of time in Kashi, an ancient Indian city which is also known as Banaras or Varanasi. The sounds of Varanasi have the ability to touch your soul. Its atmosphere is filled with the divine ripples and vibrations which can so easily raise your consciousness and elevate you spiritually.

For thousands of years, India's cultural heritage has attracted countless visitors who have come to experience these vibrations, and in the process, many have transformed their mind, body and soul.

But is it true that most of India's youth is innocently unaware of their own living heritage?

India's fast industrialisation and the increasing dominance of western commercial monoculture have prompted many Indians to join the race in which instant gratification and temporary treatments are overshadowing a permanent cure.

As a result, many are not even equipped with the fine-tuned senses that are required in order to benefit from their own golden heritage, and to deeply experience this magical land that has touched and transformed so many lives globally.

But is India fighting back and doing something to protect and preserve its cultural heritage?

In 1977, IIT Delhi Professor Kiran Seth founded an organisation called SPICMACAY which aimed to promote India's traditional music and culture.

Today, SPICMACAY has become a massive movement. Every year, it conducts thousands of events and culture workshops across the country.

For his exceptional contribution to the arts, Kiran Seth was awarded the 'Padma Shri' by the government of India.

Organising yoga workshops, theatre shows, lectures, conventions, musical fests, craft workshops, SPICMACAY is doing everything to familiarise the youth of India with their own country.

Their primary target is schools and colleges as it is the young kids and students who will be the audience of tomorrow.

SPICMACAY is a voluntary movement with about 2000 volunteers. Retired people, young professionals, teachers, housewives, students…it is the sheer dedication of these volunteers which has brought the organisation to where it is today.

Today, India is home to many thousands of cultural organisations that promote one or the other aspect of its cultural heritage and diversity.

THIRTEEN

DOES INDIA HOLD THE ANSWERS TO WORLD'S PROBLEMS?

SO, WITH all that India has, as a global community, can we also benefit from India's intellectual knowledge systems?

Well, India can definitely offer stability. I will classify that broadly into two types:

a) Environmental stability –

If we continue to promote the high ecological footprint generating lifestyle of an average American or a Scandinavian, we need many Earths. Have we chosen the wrong role models for ourselves? It's time to wake up, we can't afford that anymore.

Unfortunately, the western growth model – work – earn – spend is being blindly adopted in many developing nations including India.

This is taking us towards over-exploitation of resources,

pollution, global warming and greed-driven consumerism. The answer to that problem can be found in India's traditional concept of Aparigraha.

Aparigraha can also help in removing poverty, hunger and managing food wastage. In addition, the traditional Indian joint family system can lead to a more environmental-friendly practice of shared usage of resources. In a way, aren't we already suggesting that when we promote the so called new age idea of 'sharing economy'?

In addition, sustainable ideas like 'reuse-recycle-repair' pre-exist in the traditional Indian system and need to be revived. Those who are willing to switch to a low carbon footprint using plant – based diet can also benefit from India's vast variety of plant-based cuisine.[1]

b) Emotional stability –

From undemocratic and non-pluralistic ideas like the religious conquest of the entire world, to wars and broken families, an emotionally stable mind can only offer unrest at its best.

A nation whose people have better emotional stability are less likely to suffer from anger, greed, jealousy and all form of crime and abuse. This can also lead to stability in families, harmony between communities, resulting in the overall improved productivity and efficiency of a nation.

India's intangible cultural heritage can offer lots of solutions, especially to the communities which are more vulnerable to mental illness.

---

1 Lund University, https://www.lunduniversity.lu.se/article/the-four-lifestyle-choices-that-most-reduce-your-carbon-footprint.
WWF Report, Appetite for Destruction.

For instance, the lifetime depression prevalence in the white population is higher than in every other ethnic group in the United States.[2]

White Americans are also more likely to die by suicide than people of other ethnic groups, says the American Psychiatric Association.

The 2016 Yoga in America Study, which was conducted by Yoga Journal and Yoga Alliance found that yoga practitioners are more likely to have 'a good sense of balance' and are keener to 'give back to community'. They also become 'highly concerned about their health and the community's health.' Half of practitioners 'live green and eat sustainably'.

The relation of yoga and meditation with mental health and increased productivity is well known. In addition, Indian Dharmic knowledge traditions like Yoga and Ayurveda are also known for reducing health care costs – a rising problem in the western nations.

The American psychologist Lisa Miller has recognised the significance of spirituality in her work. She has also explored the scientific link between spirituality and health. She observes:

Children with a positive and an active relationship to spirituality:

- are 40 per cent less likely to use and abuse substances
- are 60 per cent less likely to be depressed as teenagers
- are 80 per cent less likely to have dangerous or unprotected sex

(Source: The Spiritual Child).

---

2 Depression in Racial and Ethnic Minorities: the Impact of Nativity and Discrimination – Henna Budhwani, Kristine Ria Hearld, Daniel Chavez-Yenter.

Through the help of cutting-edge research, she has explained the importance of spirituality in a child's mental and physical health and what parents can do to shape modern youth.

There is absolutely no doubt that India is the epicenter of our planet's spirituality. Perhaps, there is no civilisation in the world which has focused so much on inner exploration.

India's Dharmic traditions encourage people to focus on conquering their own mind and reject the idea of conquering the world. In Dharmic traditions, the ultimate goal is to conquer oneself. On the other hand, there are many ideologies that have had their entire focus on conquering the world.

Any ideology (religious, non-religious or scientific) which believes in global conquest can never be truly people and pluralism friendly. The idea of global conquest is against the principles on which institutions like the United Nations are built upon. In a modern, progressive and diverse global society, the ideas of conquering the globe should have no place. It should not matter what religions you follow or what non-religious or scientific ideas you have... what matters more is if your idea or your religion is making you a better person.

Shouldn't we stop running behind a temporary relief and instead seek/look for a permanent cure that lies within?

In Indian parlance, self-questioning and inner exploration are highly encouraged. That is why self-admiration and self-criticism are excessively seen in the Indian society. This not only helps to find the solutions for the problems that lie within and without, but also, it helps to ignite independent and unopinionated thinking with a deep sense of individual-inner contentment.

Based on the core philosophy of India's spiritual heritage, if we can encourage more people to focus on inward domain, we should be able to reduce all sort of crimes and wrongdoings globally.

We also need to understand that *us* and *me* are not two different things. They are co-related. A healthy Society can be formed only if there are healthy individuals. Each individual must be healed and protected. The emotional, spiritual and physical nourishment that an individual can receive within one's family is probably the most efficient and economical way of healing a society...and if these things are not taken care of, there can be emotional and financial consequences. At a micro level, we need to look at a typical family structure, which consists of loved ones.

A survey by India's NFHS has revealed that the teenagers who get out of homes at a very young age are more likely to develop habits like consuming alcohol or consuming tobacco

In the USA, a study by Columbia University indicated that having a family dinner together helps the kids in staying away from substance abuse etc.[3]

Substance abuse is directly related to additional economic burden, crime, troubled relationships and loss of productivity. No society can afford that.

India has arrived on the centerstage as one of the largest growth engines in the world, and the world's largest democracy looks all set to play a key role in shaping the future of our world.

But it does remain to be seen if Indians are able to be rational and analytical in their approach without disrespecting the valuable elements in their own heritage, traditional knowledge systems, and cultures.

---

3 The Importance of Family Dinners IV, September 2007, National Center on Addiction and Substance Abuse at Columbia University (CASA).

It also remains to be seen if they can take lessons and inspirations from their history and use that wisdom in building their future while learning and adopting the best global practices.

We shouldn't forget that the countries which were never colonised will not easily understand what it means to suffer from a post-colonial identity crisis. India may have its imperfections and shortcomings and in this process of post-colonial rebuilding, it will make its share of mistakes and it will learn from them.

Perhaps we also need to learn how to build a relation with Indians on equal terms, with mutual respect, without feeling superior or inferior, while focusing a bit more on ourselves to address our own shortcomings.

Appeal To Contribute To My Work

Hi, my name is Karolina Goswami. The book that you have just read is a result of many years of hard work. Many important facts and statistics which often surface through my investigative work are not known in the mainstream. I was not born in India but, through my logical reasoning, I have worked tirelessly to improve the way Indians are perceived globally.

Such research-based work involves years of hard work and requires a massive effort to compile information and collect data.

As long as the global community is able to understand India's complex layers and become more accommodating for both Indians and India, which is also now my new home, I will continue to feel satisfied.

Please come forward and support this mission financially. With your financial support, I will be able to achieve results faster.

Please drop an email to learn how you can financially support this mission:

Email: indiaindetails@gmail.com
www.indiaindetails.com

About The Author

Karolina Goswami comes from the south eastern region of Poland. She holds a master's degree from the Rzeszów University of Technology and is a production engineer by training.

Driven by her passion to provide a broader perspective to the sides of India that are not fully known or understood, Karolina Goswami is known for creating data-driven non-political content (documentary films, short videos) which ignites independent thinking and logical reasoning.

Her well-researched short videos and documentary films are regularly uploaded on the Social media Channel – India In Details.

'India In Details' has nearly 400,000 subscribers on YouTube and more than 500,000 followers on Facebook, as of October 2019.

In her journey as a filmmaker, Karolina Goswami has delivered nearly 100 episodes on a variety of subjects related to India and Indians. Cumulatively, her episodes have had more than 100 million views on various social media platforms.

From India's premier academic institution – IIT Kharagpur, to the country's tourism, healthcare, economy, environment and its cultural and spiritual heritage, her episodes have covered a very wide spectrum. She has also highlighted the success stories of overseas Indians and the challenges faced by them.

In order to build a more accurate perception of India in the country of her birth, Karolina Goswami has started a painstaking and mammoth task of visiting the primary schools, secondary schools and universities in Poland to give lectures or speeches on India. These workshops are helping the next Polish generation to become more informed, more accepting and better prepared to live in an increasing globalised world – in which India is expected to play a key role.